PADDINGTON
to the
MERSEY

In a scene which epitomises both the majestic grandeur of the Great Western Railway and the importance of the Birmingham main line. No. 6000 *King George V* storms past the loco sheds south of Leamington Spa and into Whitnash cutting, at the start of twelve miles of almost continuous climbing to the summit south of Fenny Compton. The date is 1938, and the GWR is at its zenith.

ENGLAND and BELFAST,
Via LIVERPOOL,
and the Belfast Steam Ship Company's

New EXPRESS .
TWIN SCREW . .
STEAMERS. . . .

Open Sea Passage,
$5\frac{1}{2}$ Hours.

DAILY
(Sundays excepted).

Accelerated Train Service in both directions between LONDON and LIVERPOOL by the New Route, via BICESTER.

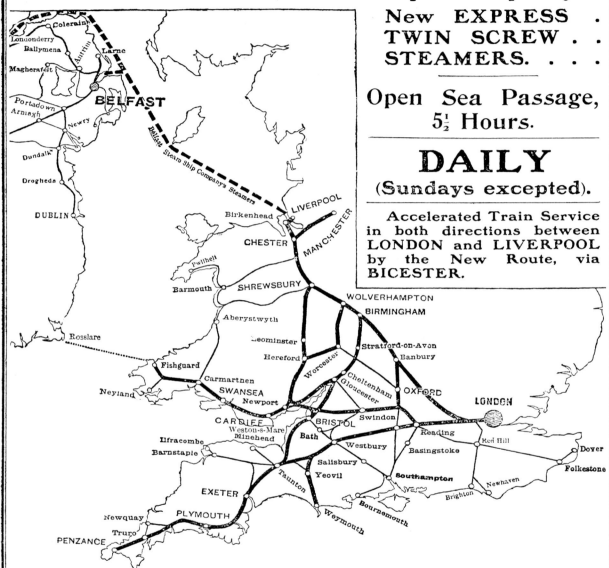

TRAIN AND BOAT SERVICES.

	Week Days.	Mons. and Thurs. only.		Saturdays and Sundays excepted.	Wednes-days.		Saturdays.	
	p.m.	a.m.		p.m.	p.m.		p.m.	p.m.
LONDON (Paddington) ...... dep.	4 0	11 5	Londonderry ...... dep. about	.	1 K 0		...	1 K 0
Birmingham (Snow Hill) . ,,	6 5	2 28	BELFAST (Donegall Quay) ... dep.	9 0	...		9 30	...
Wolverhampton (Low Level) ,,	6 29	2 57	LIVERPOOL—					Sundays.
Cardiff . . . . . ,,	4 15	12 38	(Princes Landing Stage or { arr.	a.m.	a.m.		a.m.	a.m.
Newport . . . . . ,,	4 37	1 2	Princes Dock) { abt.	6 30	7 9		7 9	7 0
Plymouth (Millbay) . . ,,	12 32	8 45		a.m.	a.m.	a.m.		a.m.
Bristol (Temple Meads) ...... ,,	4 10	12 45	Liverpool (Landing Stage) . dep.	8 0	8 50	8 0		8 20
Shrewsbury . . . . . ,,	7 26	3 50	Shrewsbury . . . . arr.	9 58	10 54	9 58		11 32
Liverpool (Landing Stage) ... arr.	9 30	5 50	Bristol (Temple Meads) . . ,,	. . .	5 43	1 57	1 57	Thursdays.	7 43
LIVERPOOL—			Plymouth (Millbay) . . . . . ,,	. . .	5 43	5 43		4*53
(Princes Landing Stage or		p.m.	Newport . . . . ,,	. . .	1 38	1 38		8 29
Princes Dock) Steamer . dep.	10 0	7 K 0	Cardiff . . . . ,,	. . .	2 1	2 1		8 52
BELFAST (Donegall Quay) { arr.	a.m.		Wolverhampton (Low Level) ,,	10 46	. . .	10 46		12 50
{ abt.	6 0		Birmingham (Snow Hill) ... ,,	11 10	. . .	11 10		1 36
Londonderry . . . { arr.		p.m.	LONDON (Paddington) . . ,,	1 25	. . .	1 25		5 45
{ abt.		1 N 0						

K—Or as soon after as tide permits.   N—Tuesdays and Fridays.   *—Monday Morning.

RESTAURANT CAR TRAINS.
FOR FURTHER PARTICULARS SEE PAGE 180.

2

PADDINGTON to the MERSEY

by
Dr. R. Preston Hendry MRCS, LRCP, BA(Cantab)
&
R. Powell Hendry LLB, FCA

Oxford Publishing Co.

A catalogue record for this book is available from the British Library

ISBN 0-86093-442-X

Library of Congress catalog card number
91-73004

Oxford Publishing Co. is part of the
Haynes Publishing Group
Sparkford, Near Yeovil, Somerset, BA22 7JJ

Haynes Publications Inc.
861 Lawrence Drive, Newbury Park, California 91320, USA.

Printed by: J. H. Haynes & Co.Ltd
Typeset in Times Medium Roman 9/10pt.

Publisher's note: A number of the photographs in this album are from original prints of poor quality, but have been included because of their rarity, historical interest and importance.

Contents

Acknowledgements & References

We have consulted a wide variety of historical works, and contemporary GWR and BR official documents in preparing this portrait. Many of the photographs are from the authors' cameras. Others are from negatives in our archives, including work by J.N.Maskelyne and H.J.Stretton Ward. Much invaluable data has come from Stanford Jacobs, 'Jake' who, most unusually, combines outstanding knowledge of signalling operation and motive power into one. Our last acknowledgement is a sad one; it is to Mrs Elaine Hendry SRN QAIMNS/R (1906-1986), wife and mother, without whose patience and willingness to let us film locomotives, trains, signal boxes and stations, and to put up with the piles of material strewn about the house, neither this, nor any of our previous books, could ever have been written.

Dr Robert Preston Hendry

On 18th October 1991, as this book was at proof stage, Dr Robert Preston Hendry, MRCS, LRCP, BA(Cantab), RAMC (Retd), passed away. He was born in Crosby, Liverpool in 1912, and his earliest memories of railways were on Merseyside and the Isle of Man. His parents later moved to the Midlands. He was a founder member of Cambridge University Railway Society, and after qualifying in medicine was posted to Egypt in 1939, getting to know the Egyptian State Railways. He became Medical Officer to 1st Royal Tank Regiment, which was to become a part of the legendary *Desert Rats*, and with 131 Field Ambulance. He was mentioned in dispatches in 1941.

After the war, he returned to civilian medicine, campaigning on many safety issues. From the 1960s, he was active in railway preservation in the Isle of Man, and was joint author of ten books on railways, covering the Isle of Man, the LMS, LNWR and GWR.

In recognition of his services to railway preservation, electric locomotive No. 23 of the Manx Electric Railway is to be named *Dr R. Preston Hendry*.

Preface

In writing any book upon the Great Western Railway, other than on perhaps the most abstruse topic possible, the modern author risks the charge that nothing new has been said. There is much truth in this, for the bones of Great Western history were laid bare decades ago, but in the vast, and still growing mass of GWR literature, there are still areas which are not well covered, or where the reader must search diligently to gain an overall impression. Locomotives, carriages, wagons, stations, signal boxes have all been described. It is relatively easy to discover the story of the Great Western main line from Paddington to Bristol and the West Country, yet if one wishes to make the journey – in print – from Paddington to Oxford, Banbury,

Leamington Spa, Birmingham, Shrewsbury, Chester and Birkenhead, it is a different matter.

It was the realisation of that gap which prompted this book. Both authors have particular memories of the Great Western line to Birmingham and the Mersey. In 1938, one of the authors used it to return from his honeymoon to resume duty with the Royal Army Medical Corps. More than twenty years later, the second of the authors spent happy hours with schoolfriends watching and photographing trains on the Birmingham main line.

We have enjoyed putting this portrait of a great main line together; we hope you enjoy reading it.

Introduction

The words 'Great Western' summon up an image of engines in Middle Chrome Green, with copper capped chimneys and polished brightwork, of chocolate and cream carriages, of distinctive lower quadrant signals, 'Micas' and 'Toads'. The image is correct, but paradoxically, it is normally seen in a very narrow context. To the majority of those to whom the words 'Great Western' mean so much, that image is confined to the London and Bristol main line, and the West Country. Paddington, Swindon, Box Tunnel, Temple Meads, Dainton, Dawlish and Laira are all a part of the fabric, but the wider Great Western is not. This is strange, for none of the other great railway companies is seen in so limited a perspective. To Midland devotees, the Midland is not just the Settle & Carlisle, any more than the LNWR is the 'London & Birmingham' or West Coast Main Line.

This strange dichotomy, in which much of the Great Western is all but ignored by its most faithful devotees was brought home to the authors when reading one recent work on the railway. Views of Bristol and the West abounded, but scarcely a handful of views showed what lay north of Didcot. It was as if an 'iron curtain' had descended over much of a great railway, and that one of its trunk routes, over which much effort and many millions of pounds were expended, was consigned to obscurity.

Paddington to the Mersey is a portrait of that trunk route, a line which the Great Western itself valued highly, and which it made every effort to develop, but which has been all but forgotten. Why this should be so, is hard to envisage. The birth of the GWR route to the Mersey, which began not all that long after the Bristol line was finished, is as full of drama as its more famous predecessor. In some ways it was more so, for the Great Western faced the opposition of the London & North Western and the Midland railways, and its success, in driving a main line through to the Mersey is all the more remarkable. The giants of early Great Western history leave their mark on the Birmingham main line, Brunel and Gooch. In later days, it could match the grandeur of the West of England line class for class; 'Kings' and 'Castles', 'Halls', 'Stars' and 'Saints', rode its metals. Engines blasted their way up to Hatton or Harbury in displays of power which could match Dainton or Whiteball. 'Aberdares', 28xxs, 'RODs' and 56xxs provided a display of freight power which the West of England could not match indeed! In 1947, one of the lesser Wolverhampton Division sheds, Banbury, had almost

as many 2-8-0s as the whole of the Newton Abbot division put together. Another measure of the sheer hard slogging work to be found on the Birmingham main line, was that at its depots, from Banbury to Birkenhead, the Wolverhampton Division deployed more of the 56xx tanks than the whole of the Newton Abbot and Bristol divisions put together. Indeed Leamington Spa, a quite minor shed, could equal those two whole divisions, and if ever an engine was tailor-made for tough work it was the 56xx. Not even the most devoted admirer of Swindon could call the 56xx a pretty locomotive; purposeful would be a far better word. They were devised for the murderous conditions of the Welsh valleys, and their appearance on the Birmingham main line speaks volumes. Perhaps we have the best of both worlds, the glamour of the West of England, with its high stepping 'Stars', 'Saints' and 'Kings', and the down-to-earth slogging of the Valleys!

In the pages which follow, we have sought to recapture that excitement, and 28xxs and 56xxs share the limelight with 'Castles' and 'Kings', for that is what it was like. Engines are seen at work, and at rest. We did not want to make this merely a record of locomotives or trains, and stations and signal boxes make their appearance. As with its motive power, the Birmingham main line could hold its own with any section of the Great Western. We have naturally traced the route in outline from Paddington to Didcot, and what a splendid route it is, but our emphasis has been on the old line north of Didcot, and the splendid cut-off through High Wycombe, Princes Risborough and Bicester. Shrewsbury, Wrexham and Birkenhead make an appearance, and with them, the maze of tracks which made up the Birkenhead Dock Railways for although these were largely owned by the Mersey Docks & Harbour Board, GWR and LMS engines worked over them and the docks were a magnet which drew the Great Western northwards.

One of the themes we have tried to draw out is the diversity of this route, with its Brunellian train shed at Banbury or Brunellian 'italianate' at Harbury. They rub shoulders with pagodas at Denham Golf Course, or GW 'modernism' at Leamington Spa. In the case of Leamington, we have depicted what a major rebuilding was really like, mess and all, for all too often, 'official' photographs are taken at suitable intervals with some discreet tidying up beforehand!

Apart from the main lines themselves, we have sought to cover a number of the branches. We have omitted the well-known branches on the old main line as far as Didcot, so our first diversion is Abingdon. Blenheim and the Princes Risborough lines follow, whilst we journey to Stratford-on-Avon also. If we are to avoid becoming sidetracked too often, we must be careful, so the maze of lines west from Birmingham to Shrewsbury are omitted, as these were in many cases more closely associated with the Worcester Division than the Birmingham main line, irrespective of which division they actually fell in. We have not felt it right to include other 'main lines' such as the Oxford, Worcester & Wolverhampton for they form a different story, but we hope our byways will give a sufficient flavour of the lines which fed into the Great Western route from Paddington to the Mersey.

In point of time, we have ranged from the Edwardian era to recent days, though with an emphasis from the 1920s to the 1950s. The last piece of the jigsaw puzzle was not put in place by the GWR until 1910, and it is from there on that we have portrayed it. Over sixty different classes of motive power appear, and if space was unlimited, the list could be extended. We had intended to include a 57xx, but in the end decided that 655, 850 and 2021 class pannier tanks were far rarer birds. Over 80 different stations, junctions and other interesting locations are covered, many with several views.

Opposite top The roof board of this diagram C77 compartment third reads 'PADDINGTON BIRMINGHAM SHREWSBURY CHESTER AND BIRKENHEAD'. She is in the final GWR carriage livery with the arms of London and Bristol flanked by 'GREAT' and 'WESTERN'. The date of the illustration is 1949, and the adjacent vehicle bears a BR number W920. This was a Hawksworth diagram C82 third, just a year old when this illustration was taken.

Below No. 6004 *King George III* is at rest in Paddington's No. 10 main line arrivals platform, her 123 mile journey from Wolverhampton done. The fireman has already removed one of the headlamps, and is largely obscured by the smoke box as he stows it on the side brackets. Soon the locomotive will back out of the station for servicing, prior to returning to her home depot, Wolverhampton, Stafford Road, which boasted half a dozen 'Kings' at the time of this early-fifties portrait.

Opposite below It is April 1930, and No. 3577, a Belpaire boilered 3571 class 0-4-2T, is in charge of a Chester District local passenger working at Birkenhead (Woodside) station. In the foreground is one of the gas replenishment hoses which were once a feature of major termini. The station with its LNWR signals and sombre rock-faced stone walling, is a strange environment for a Great Western engine.

Historical Review

The Great Western routes from Paddington to the Mersey were not the outcome of a single master plan, but in common with other trunk routes, of piecemeal growth. Their history has been covered many times, most notably in MacDermot's classic *History of the Great Western Railway*. However the sheer volume of detail can obscure the salient facts, hence this outline summary.

Paddington-Didcot Authorised on 31st August 1835 as part of the GWR Bristol main line. Opened Paddington-Maidenhead on 4th June 1838; to Twyford 1st July 1839; Reading, 30th March 1840 and to Steventon (West of Didcot) 1st June 1840.

Didcot-Oxford Various GWR-associated proposals fell through prior to the GWR-backed Oxford Railway Co., which was authorised on 11th April 1843. Merged into GWR 10th May 1844; line opened 12th June 1844 (also first Didcot station).

Oxford & Rugby Railway Co. In the 1840s, Rugby was a key point for all routes north, with the Midland Counties Railway joining the London & Birmingham. The O&RR was the GWR-backed victor of rival broad and 'narrow' gauge schemes. Authorised on 4th August 1845; amalgamated into GWR on 14th May 1846; opened Oxford to Banbury 2nd September 1850 and Banbury-Fenny Compton on 1st October 1852. Fenny Compton to Rugby was not built due to change in the railway political situation.

Birmingham & Oxford Junction Railway The B&OJR arose through Grand Junction Railway suspicions towards the London & Birmingham, and the GJR wish to secure an alternative route to London, via the GWR. As a result of GJR 'flirtation' with GWR, the GJR was able to conclude advantageous merger terms with the Manchester & Birmingham and London & Birmingham railways to form the London & North Western Railway in 1846. Although abandoned by its 'ally', the GWR persevered alone with the B&OJR, which was authorised from a junction with the O&RR at Fenny Compton to a junction with the LNWR near Curzon Street, Birmingham on 3rd August 1846. A further act, of the same date, permitted a further line to Birmingham (Snow Hill). B&OJR was vested in the GWR on 31st August 1848 and opened Fenny Compton-Snow Hill on 1st October 1852. The link to the LNWR was not completed. At one time the Company nearly fell into LNWR hands!

Birmingham, Wolverhampton & Dudley Railway A GWR-backed line to run from Birmingham (Snow Hill) to a junction with the Oxford, Worcester & Wolverhampton Railway at Priestfield, Wolverhampton. Authorised on 3rd August 1846 and vested in the GWR 31st August 1848. As the GWR hoped to negotiate with the LNWR and obtain access to Wolverhampton, via their Stour Valley line, construction was held up until 1851. Opened Birmingham to Priestfield on 14th November 1854.

Oxford, Worcester & Wolverhampton Railway Authorised 4th August 1845 between Oxford and Bushbury Junction (with LNWR). Opened in sections from 1850, the two mile section from Priestfield to Wolverhampton (Cannock Road) was opened to passengers on 1st July 1854.

Shrewsbury & Birmingham Railway The S&BR was a local concern, initially with L&BR affinities, but lost L&B support on formation of the LNWR. The Wolverhampton to Birmingham section was in competition to GWR and LNWR backed schemes, and failed, the S&BR being granted running powers over the LNW-associated Stour Valley line instead. The section between Shrewsbury and Wellington was to be jointly built with the Shropshire Union Railways & Canal Co., only the section from Wellington to Wolverhampton being S&BR solely. Authorised 3rd August 1846. Opened Shrewsbury to Oakengates 1st June 1849 and Oakengates to Wolverhampton (LNWR) 12th November 1849. There was prolonged hostility with the LNWR, and the company merged into the GWR on 1st September 1854. The SUR was leased to the LNWR from 1847, and although it technically survived until the Grouping in 1923, the Wellington-Shrewsbury section was effectively LNWR and GWR Joint.

Shrewsbury & Chester Railway The S&CR was an amalgamation of the North Wales Mineral Railway, authorised from Chester to Wrexham in 1844, and the Shrewsbury, Oswestry & Chester Junction Railway, authorised in 1845, the two merging in 1846. The line from Ruabon to Saltney Junction, just outside Chester on the Chester & Holyhead Railway (later LNWR) opened on 4th November 1846, and from Ruabon to Shrewsbury on 14th October 1848. In common with the S&BR, the S&CR was merged into the GWR from 1st September 1854.

Birkenhead Railway The BR was also an amalgamation of two companies, the Chester & Birkenhead, which opened on 23rd September 1840, and Birkenhead Lancashire & Cheshire Junction Railway, which was authorised in 1846, merged with the C&BR in 1847 using the longer title, and opened a line from Chester to near Warrington on 18th December 1850. After nearly falling wholly in the GWR camp in 1851-52, the railway was retitled the Birkenhead Railway on 1st August 1859 and was transferred jointly to the GWR and LNWR on 1st January 1860.

Acton-Ashendon Junction Railway As the first stage of a 'cut-off' a new line was authorised in 1897 from near Old Oak to High Wycombe, on the GWR Maidenhead-Wycombe-Princes Risborough-Oxford branch, which was to be upgraded, and from 'Risboro to Grendon Underwood (junction with GCR). The GW & GC Joint Committee was set up 1899, to which the High Wycombe-Princes Risborough section was transferred. The section from Ashendon to Grendon Underwood became GCR-only. Opened to goods on 20th November 1905 and to passengers 2nd April 1906. (High Wycombe-Risborough had been opened as a single track branch in August 1862.)

Ashendon to Aynho 18m final link of cut-off from GW & GC Joint at Ashendon to Oxford-Banbury line at Aynho, south of Banbury. Authorised 1905; opened to goods 4th April 1910; opened to passengers 1st July 1910.

Paddington to Leamington Spa

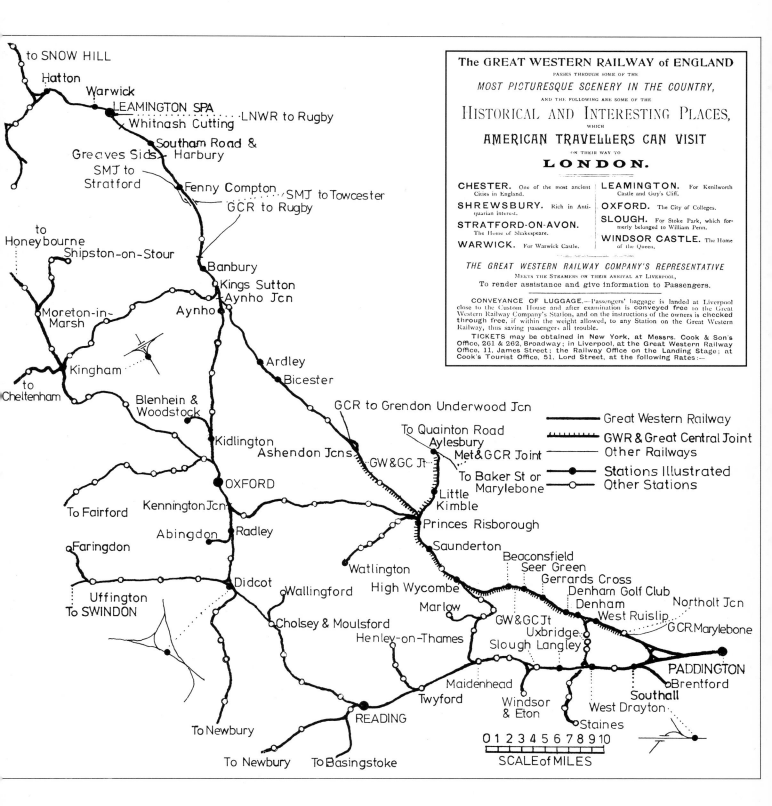

The GREAT WESTERN RAILWAY of ENGLAND
PASSES THROUGH SOME OF THE
MOST PICTURESQUE SCENERY IN THE COUNTRY,
AND THE FOLLOWING ARE SOME OF THE
HISTORICAL AND INTERESTING PLACES,
WHICH
AMERICAN TRAVELLERS CAN VISIT
ON THEIR WAY TO
LONDON.

CHESTER. One of the most ancient Cities in England.

SHREWSBURY. Rich in Antiquarian interest.

STRATFORD-ON-AVON. The Home of Shakespeare.

WARWICK. For Warwick Castle.

LEAMINGTON. For Kenilworth Castle and Guy's Cliff.

OXFORD. The City of Colleges.

SLOUGH. For Stoke Park, which formerly belonged to William Penn.

WINDSOR CASTLE. The Home of the Queen.

THE GREAT WESTERN RAILWAY COMPANY'S REPRESENTATIVE
MEETS THE STEAMERS ON THEIR ARRIVAL AT LIVERPOOL,
To render assistance and give information to Passengers.

CONVEYANCE OF LUGGAGE.—Passengers' baggage is landed at Liverpool close to the Custom House and after examination is conveyed free to the Great Western Railway Company's Station, and on the instructions of the owners is checked through free, if within the weight allowed, to any Station on the Great Western Railway, thus saving passengers all trouble.

TICKETS may be obtained in New York, at Messrs. Cook & Son's Office, 261 & 262, Broadway; in Liverpool, at the Great Western Railway Office, 11, James Street; the Railway Office on the Landing Stage; at Cook's Tourist Office, 51, Lord Street, at the following Rates:—

Great Western Railway

GWR & Great Central Joint

Other Railways

● Stations Illustrated

○ Other Stations

0 1 2 3 4 5 6 7 8 9 10
SCALE of MILES

9

Paddington

Above The three great spans of Brunel's original train shed at Paddington date from 1854-55, and constitute one of the most spacious terminals from the steam age. By the date of this view, 8th August 1965, the proud reign of Great Western steam was drawing to a close.

Below Two 'Kings' and a 'Hall' make ready to depart under Bishop's Road bridge in an early post-war scene. The centre locomotive, Stafford Road's No. 6005 *King George II,* carries the 985 reporting number of a Wolverhampton express.

Above Looking west from platform 8 at the maze of tracks stretching out towards the twin-span Westbourne Terrace bridge, it becomes apparent how Paddington could handle traffic for the West of England, South Wales, the Midlands and Merseyside so smoothly.

Below An "aircraft" 'Castle', No. 5081 *Lockheed Hudson* drifts into Paddington in early BR days. The goods depot owes its strange profile to station improvements in 1928-32, when it was slightly cut back. The enamel 'Tangye Pumps' advertisement seems rather lonely in that expanse of plain wall!

Ranelagh Bridge

Above With its west end location, well away from the 'City', the GWR took a keen interest in inner London lines such as the Metropolitan, and from 1865, the Hammersmith & City Railway paralleled the GWR from Westbourne Park to Paddington. In 1867, it became GW & Metropolitan joint. From its platforms on the north side of the line at Royal Oak, it was possible to obtain an excellent view of the engine sidings at Ranelagh Bridge. These were used to service engines from the out-stations. In this early sixties transition scene, two of the short lived "Blue Pullman" sets share the yard with various steam engines, including 'Castle' class No. 7000 *Viscount Portal*. The luxurious diesel sets provided prestige services to Bristol, South Wales and Birmingham/Wolverhampton. In 1962 there were two runs each way on the Birmingham line, the First Class Pullman supplement between Paddington and Snow Hill being 11 shillings (55p) single.

Southall

Below The Great Western Railway was originally envisaged as the 'Bristol & London Rail Road', and wayside communities were of little note. As a result, the line swept majestically west-south-west from Paddington, and when the first 22 miles as far as Maidenhead opened in June 1838, Southall was not deemed worthy of a station for some months. Although consideration had been given to a branch to Oxford, pre-occupation with the Bristol traffic meant that when the Great Western began to expand towards the Cotswolds and the Midlands, that its route was, to say the least, circuitous. For almost sixty years, until 1910, Birmingham services rubbed shoulders with Bristol traffic as far as Didcot. A 'Warship' class diesel, with the early small yellow warning panels, recalls the relatively short-lived diesel hydraulic era, as she hammers through Southall en route to Paddington with a mid-day express. Note the GWR ATC ramp on the 'down' main.

West Drayton

Above Forty years after the GWR ceased to exist, the classic lines of its station architecture were still apparent at West Drayton.

Langley

Below Tower-like hipped roofs, truncated at the top and surmounted by ornate ironwork, characterised many stations on the Reading line, although the individual treatment varied greatly. Langley in Buckinghamshire was the work of Lancaster Owen, and dates from 1878. Happily it still stands today.

Reading

Didcot

Above Dean 2361 class 0-6-0 double framed goods No. 2369 awaits departure with a local passenger working from the Basingstoke/Newbury bays at the west end of Reading about 1931. Unlike the 'Dean goods', the 2361s were seldom used on passenger turns. Note the inspection pit in the adjacent road.

Below Today, Didcot shed, located in the divergence of the Bristol and Oxford lines, is a thriving preservation centre, but in 1931 it was a busy shed. On the left is a 2361 class goods engine, while in the centre is 'Bulldog' class 4-4-0, No. 3448 *Kingfisher*.

Above Radley, midway between Didcot and Oxford, was opened in 1873, almost thirty years after the Oxford line. It was built in conjunction with alterations to the Abingdon branch, which had been opened in 1856. The buildings were in red brick, with limestone quoins and plinth.

Radley

Below This 1953 study of the north end of Radley and entrance to the 'down' relief, depicts the timber post starter formerly on the branch platform with route indicator, and the 'down' platform starters on an early tubular post bracket.

PASSENGERS ARE REQUESTED TO CROSS THE LINE BY THE BRIDGE

Oxford

Above As the original Oxford Railway terminus of 1844 was unsuitable as a through station, it was replaced in 1852. Its successor, seen in 1956, stood for 120 years. Great Western timber buildings lasted!

Left Oxford was invariably a hive of activity, for apart from Birmingham and 'OW&W' services, branch trains ran to Fairford, Princes Risborough and Blenheim & Woodstock. 0-4-2T No. 1437 and trailer No. W153, former steam railcar No. 68, are seen in the 'up' platform in 1951.

Below As Oxford based No. 5960 *Saint Edmund Hall* is routed into the South sidings in 1950, a Southern 'King Arthur' waits a through train, and another 'Hall' moves off the 'down' sidings, right, wherein a fourth engine waits.

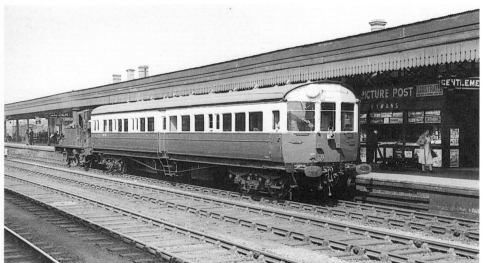

Above No. 5017 *St Donats Castle,* blows off vigorously as she enters Oxford on the 10.48am Hereford-Worcester-Oxford-Paddington on a glorious summer day in 1948. The 10.48 was one of the principal duties for Worcester's then allocation of eight 'Castles', the return working being the 4.45pm ex-Paddington. At a time when 'austerity' was still the watchword, Worcester took especial pride in its beloved 'Castles' which received specially selected coal. No. 5017 is in a transitional livery, with buffer beam number and WOS code on the angle iron, but BRITISH RAILWAYS – albeit in GW serif style – on the tender! In April 1954, this locomotive was renamed *The Gloucestershire Regiment 28th/61st* to commemorate the regiment's heroic stand at the Imjin River, during the Korean War. No. 5017 was withdrawn, from Gloucester shed, in September 1962.

Right It is 20th October 1930, and as Churchward 'County' class 4-4-0, No. 3829 *County of Merioneth* is hand signalled into the 'down' platform at Oxford, the sands of time are running out for these attractive little 4-4-0s. Between 1930 and 1933 the entire class was slaughtered, falling victim to the increasing fleet of Collett 'Hall' class 4-6-0s. Many, including No. 3829, spent their final months at Oxford, whilst others congregated a few miles north, at Leamington. The nearest two vehicles are both horse boxes, then a common sight on every type of train, from branch local to express passenger. It is a feature modellers often overlook.

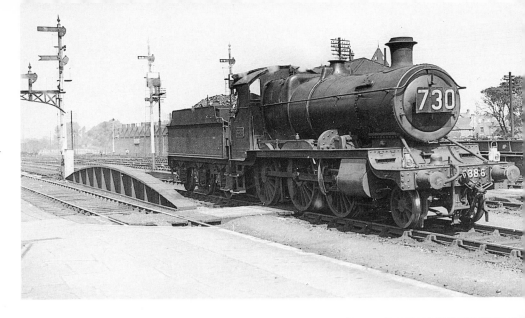

Top A 4300 class Mogul, No. 5386, has just been relieved from an 'up' express, and stands on the 'down' main, waiting a chance to go on shed. Although the date is September 1948, as yet there is nothing to betray the transition from Great Western to British Railways. The GWR backing signals, with route indicator, are particularly attractive. The building immediately to the left of No. 5386 is the two-road LNWR loco shed serving the neighbouring North Western terminus, Oxford (Rewley Road).

Centre Just to the north of Oxford station, the line was carried across the quaintly named Sheepwash Channel, which connected the Rivers Thames/Isis. A Stanier 8F 2-8-0, No. 48129 is caught on the bridge in 1964. To the left is Oxford Station North signal box, whilst the houses in Abbey Road to the right obscure the station. Oxford shed was just north of the Sheepwash Channel, surrounded by watercourses and small footbridges!

Bottom Tucked away in the dim recesses of Oxford shed was stationary boiler (No. 1152 in the 'plant' series). In the left background is one of the shed walls, its advanced state of decay being all too apparent in this scene of 16th October 1964. The hand-painted shed code is a delightful touch, for one could scarcely imagine this boiler straying far from its home shed!

Above A careworn 'Dean Goods', No. 2568, heads a class F through fast freight, southbound along the 'up' main in 1948. No. 2568, one of the last 'Dean Goods' to be built, in 1898, survived until the 'purge' of the type in 1953, and the onslaught of the BR Standard Class 2 2-6-0s, which initially, were much inferior engines!

Kidlington

Right Kidlington was the first passenger station north of Oxford on the Banbury line, and the junction for the short Woodstock branch (see page 62). Train movements were controlled from a neat brick and timber signal box typical of those erected throughout the Great Western, up to the turn of the century. Note the small window panes and decorative ridge tiling.

Aynho

Upper left Aynho station, six miles south of Banbury, was in the Brunellian style with gentle sloping roof, and all-round awning. The lion's heads on the valance are a particularly ornate example of a theme found in GW stations of 1848-50. These are the 'down' buildings, looking towards Banbury in 1956.

Lower left No. 4083 *Abbotsbury Castle* approaches Aynho with a 'down' express in 1956. The Ashendon-Aynho cut-off, which joined the Oxford line just north of Aynho station is visible in the left background.

Above From 1910, passengers at Aynho station had this view of the 'down' cut-off line, carried imperiously over the Oxford lines on a single span lattice girder. In the fifties, freight was still handled and flower beds tended.

Below A '43xx' Mogul, No. 6331, heads a class C fitted freight south through Aynho in 1956. The variation in van roofs is worthy of attention by modellers, as the average model freight train is far too uniform in style, height and colour. Note the rain strips on some roofs and prominent planking on others.

The New Line

West Ruislip

It would be hard to imagine a more graphic illustration of the superb engineering standards adopted for the GW & GC Joint line than this study of West Ruislip station, with the quadruple tracks stretching as straight as an arrow as far as the eye can see. London Transport Central line services run from here to the 'city'.

Two pieces of classic railway insignia are reflected in the glazing panels on the road frontage of West Ruislip station on 16th August 1988. The London Transport 'UndergrounD' insignia is one of the best known transport devices anywhere in the world, and has guided generations of Londoners and visitors to and from the labyrinthine underground network. The survival of a British Railways 'totem' in Western Region chocolate, on the outside of an important suburban station is most surprising at such a late date, particularly one in such splendid condition. West Ruislip was called Ruislip & Ickenham until 30th June 1947. Today it is served by LT, and BR dmus from Marylebone, but the only Paddington service over the joint line is a solitary express each way to Leamington, calling at Bicester, Princes Risborough and High Wycombe.

Looking west from the 'down' platform at West Ruislip towards the functional but commodious LT/BR station buildings and overbridge. North of the station, the joint line becomes double track, and is still controlled – at the time of this 1988 view – by genuine Great Western signalling.

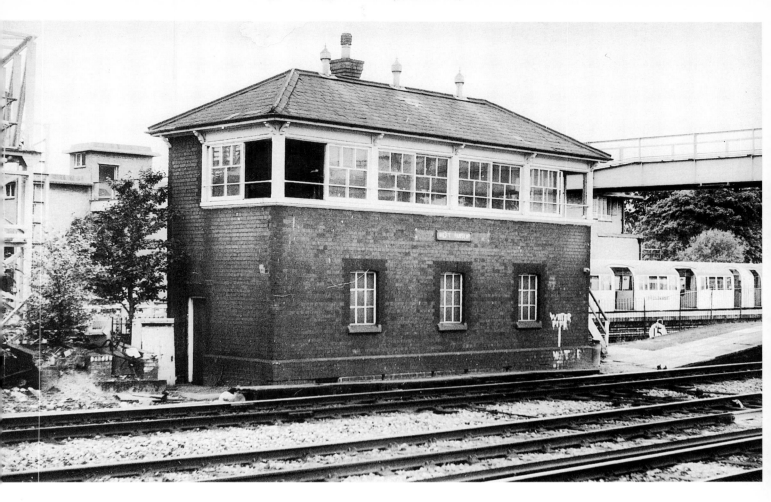

West Ruislip

Above In this age of power signalling and modern architecture, it is pleasing to discover a traditional Great Western signal box within a dozen miles of Paddington. West Ruislip box is of the standard pattern built from c1900, and shows the curious 5-pane windows adopted as standard at that time.

Denham

Below Denham station, just 14¾ miles from Paddington, still retains its rural character, although sadly, the ending of any significant express service over the joint line has robbed the station of the need for the fast tracks which were a feature of every station of any importance upon the GW & GC Joint. 'Network SouthEast' signs appear in this 1988 study.

Denham Golf Club

Above left The Great Western Railway was unwavering in its belief in the merits of country pursuits, such as hunting, shooting, fishing and golf. It became an enthusiastic devotee of steam railcars, and numerous halts or 'platforms' appeared in the early 1900s. These twin influences led to the opening of Denham Golf Club Platform on 8th August 1912. Yet another enthusiasm was for corrugated iron 'huts', the most impressive of which had a Chinese Pagoda pattern roof. A lesser variety existed, and when our fellow enthusiast, Stanford Jacobs, studied this portrait of the 'down' booking hut, his immediate quip was "I'm going to be a Pagoda when I grow up".

Above right A few stations contained obvious 'activities' in their names, such as Rifle Range or Golf Club, and it has long been the authors' wish to photograph a rifleman or golfer at the 'matching' station. Our opportunity came at Denham Golf Club on 9th August 1988. The golfer, a member of a Swedish airline crew flying into Heathrow, had not enjoyed a particularly good round, but certainly made the authors' day! Under Great Western auspices, the station was sensibly named 'Denham Golf Club Platform', but for some strange reason BR felt obliged to abolish the 'Platform', making the station appear as if it was exclusively for a private club in this instance.

Below Denham Golf Club, looking east towards Paddington on 16th August 1988, with a pair of classic pagodas. The closure of so many minor stations and appearance of 'bus shelter' structures at others, has made the pagoda a threatened species, and the survival of this trio occasioned much delight, and the sudden realisation that it is probably only the railway enthusiast who can find architectural merit and excellence in corrugated iron! Of course a flat roof, or one sloping the wrong way, would have been a different matter.

Gerrards Cross

Above One of the most attractive stations on the Joint line was Gerrards Cross, where an access road sloped down to an impressive two-storey building on the 'up' side of the line. Except in incidentals, the station buildings have hardly changed from the day they opened in April 1906 to the date of this scene, August 1988.

Below Where Great Western steam railcars once called, a BR Class 115 Driving Motor Brake Second, No. W51675 heads a 4-car Derby Suburban set towards Marylebone in August 1988. The Gerrards Cross footbridge is of such exceptional length that, most unusually, intermediate pillars are provided between the main and platform lines.

Beaconsfield

Right Beaconsfield repeated the pattern set at all the principal joint line stations, of centre fast roads flanked by platform lines. In this 1988 portrait, looking towards Birmingham, we see classic GWR buildings and footbridge, and one realises just how firmly the Great Western was in the 'driving seat' over this joint line!

Right A BR Class 3 Mogul, No. 76043 arrives in the 'down' platform with a six coach local from Marylebone. LNER devotees will recognise the unmistakeable profile of articulated suburban stock. This mixture of GWR signals, buildings and even signs, and LNER stock, gave the Joint line an attractive character. The modeller is provided with prototype justification for such improbable happenings as a Gresley A3 or Robinson A5 passing a Great Western signal box.

Below right At Beaconsfield there was a large and busy approach on the 'up' side, and a quiet secluded one on the 'down' side, which we have chosen to depict here.

Seer Green

Opposite top Golfers did well on the Joint Line, for just 4½ miles west of Denham Golf Club, another halt, Beaconsfield Golf Links was opened on 1st January 1915. Here the association was even closer, for the gate in the foreground opened onto the grounds of the golf course. Two subsequent renamings provided the station with its present name, Seer Green.

Opposite below In our second portrait of Seer Green (when named Seer Green and Jordans), we see the 'up' buildings in their entirety, the footbridge and the gate giving access to the station forecourt for non-golfing passengers. A sloping tree-lined drive dropped away to the right, joining the private drive to the golf course, ere it joined the public highway!

High Wycombe

Above High Wycombe arrived on the railway map in 1854, courtesy of the GW-associated Wycombe Railway, by means of a single track branch from Maidenhead. However, the present station is a product of the Joint era. The platforms were staggered, because of the lie of the land, and a massive brick retaining wall had to be built opposite the 'down' platform. The retaining wall is visible in the left distance in this 1988 scene looking towards the north.

Left In the fifties, Great Western station name boards and BR totems proclaimed the station's identity.

Below The 'down' side bay platform and subway, looking to the north. Subways such as this were to be found at many GWR stations and are once again neglected by the modeller. The massive retaining wall rears up behind the subway and platform.

Above The GWR platform awning, as seen on the 'down' platform at High Wycombe, was light, airy but long lasting. It has obviously lasted rather better than the clock, which is minus its hands.

Below Looking north, from the 'down' platform at High Wycombe, with the retaining wall on the right, and a banner repeater signal between the 'down' main and platform lines.

Saunderton

Above The spear-tipped railings and gate pillars with ball finials would reveal the hand of the GWR at Saunderton, north of High Wycombe, even if the 'up' buildings did not. The summit of the Joint line was between Saunderton and the next station to the north, Princes Risborough.

Princes Risborough

Below In this 1988 portrait of the 'up' buildings at Princes Risborough, we see how the awning is carried over a flat-roofed building block, and the care given to station design, with rounded or 'bull-nosed' bricks used for corners and doorways to obviate sharp edges.

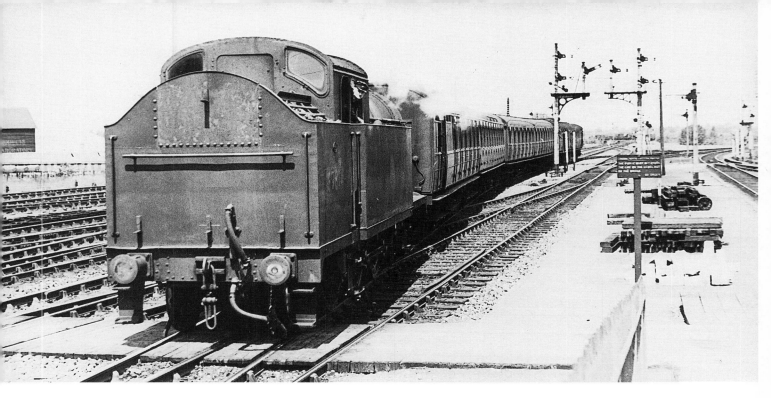

Above The two illustrations on this page, both taken within a few minutes of one another at Princes Risborough in 1951, epitomise the character of the joint line. First of all, we see a Great Central Robinson '9N' (LNER class A5) 4-6-2T, No. 69814 entering the 'up' platform with a rake of LNER suburban stock, and passing not a 'Joint' notice but an LNER one telling passengers to use the bridge rather than the barrow-way. The sign, and the mix of LNER and GC signal parts, reveals the effect of LNER responsibility for maintenance north of West Wycombe. The line to the right is the Aylesbury branch, opened as broad gauge in 1863, narrowed in 1868, and transferred from the GWR to Joint ownership on 1st July 1907.

Below From a predominantly LNER scene at Princes Risborough, we move down the platform to a wholly Great Western image, as a 'Star', No. 4049 *Princess Maud* pauses with a Paddington express. At the time, she was a Wolverhampton engine, her sisters at Stafford Road shed including Nos 4018, 4031, 4053, 4058 and 4060. The 'Castle' type outside steam pipes can be seen to good advantage. Interesting details regarding the station include the footbridge. As at Gerrards Cross, the span was so great as to require intermediate pillars between the through and platform lines. After the cut-off was downgraded in status, following closure of the GC as a through route, and electrification of the 'North Western' Birmingham line, the 'down' platform was dispensed with, and the 'up' side made bi-directional, permitting the footbridge to be removed.

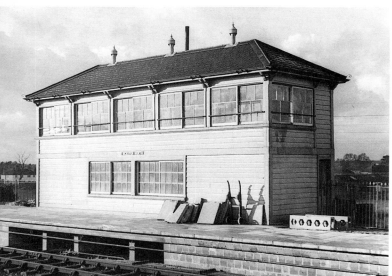

Above A '74xx' non auto-fitted pannier, probably No. 7442, one of two shedded at Slough, enters Princes Risborough with a short freight from Watlington in 1951, when just a year old. In the right distance is Princes Risborough North signal box, a pure GWR box, but with name boards mounted on the ends in LNER fashion – indicating the maintenance responsibility! The high crew costs of minute freights like this boded ill for branch lines.

Bicester

Left The final link in the GWR cut-off came with the opening of the direct line from Ashendon to Aynho in 1910. The only significant community served en route was Bicester, where an impressive station with two signal cabins was provided. This is Bicester North box in April 1951.

Left Following electrification of the West Coast Main Line, the Risborough-Aynho section was singled in 1968, Bicester retaining an 'emergency' passing loop. The main platform (originally the 'down') is portrayed in 1971.

Princes Risborough

Above This portrait of No. 6008 *King James II*, heading a Paddington express through Princes Risborough on the fast line is a natural extension of the upper illustration on the facing page. The scissors cross-over in the foreground provides connections from the 'down' platform to the 'down' main, and from the 'down' main to the Thame and Oxford branch. The North Box is on the left hand edge of the view, and a Robinson A5 class 4-6-2 tank is busy shunting on the 'down' main, between the carriages and the southbound express. The combination of a GWR box with LNER signalling was one of the delights of the Joint. The 'up' main signals are on a GC bracket, those to the right on an LNER (GE) pattern. The Aylesbury branch runs beside the two wooden huts to the right of the 'King'. The leading carriage is a Diagram D69 70ft brake third in the 'Toplight' style. The locomotive would have been carrying the short-lived BR Express Blue livery at the time of this 1951 portrait.

Ardley

Right No. 6011 *King James I* enters Ardley station, midway between Bicester and Aynho, with an express in 1951, as a '14xx' tank with auto coach take refuge in the kick-back road off the platform.

Aynho

A 'King' races north through the Oxfordshire countryside at the head of a long carmine and cream liveried express on 28th September 1956. The massive embankment, which carries the Bicester cut-off over the Oxford line, dominates this scene near Aynho Park Platform. The maximum load, to ensure maintenance of point-to-point timings for a 'King' was 500 tons between Paddington and Leamington, but only 400 tons for a Paddington-Birmingham service, due to Hatton bank. This train must be on, if not above, the limit for a through working.

Banbury

Right above A brand new 5101 class large Prairie tank, No. 5169 blows off gently by the goods shed at the south end of Banbury station. Many GWR goods depots were adorned with massive sign boards, to which individual cast letters were fixed, but here the sign is painted directly on the boarding, 'GREAT WESTERN RAILWAY' in sans serif, and 'GOODS STATION' in a serif style derived from some of the more ornate cast notices.

Right No. 6008 *King James II* makes another appearance, this time at the head of a southbound express at Banbury in 1931. The train shed, which was in the Brunellian style, dated from 1850, and £99,000 was set aside by the GWR for reconstruction of the station, the first third in 1939. The outbreak of war in 1939 led to the scheme being postponed until BR days.

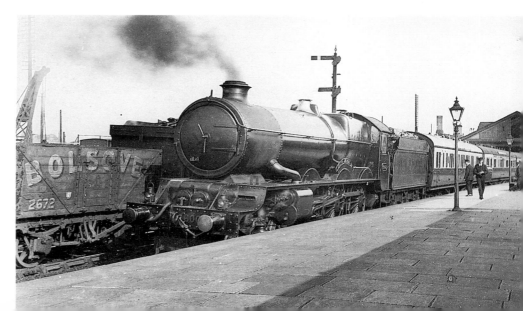

A grimy '93xx' series Mogul, No. 9316, carrying class K headcode, pilot trip, stopping freight or branch freight, sets back into the 'up' sorting sidings at the north end of Banbury station in 1952. With the connection on to the LMR just north of Banbury, the sidings were an important interchange point between the LNER and the Great Western, and were correspondingly busy. No. 9316, which was an Oxford engine in late GWR/early BR days is, most unusually, running without a safety valve casing.

A road bridge which crossed the line just north of the passenger station provided the vantage point for this portrait of Banbury station looking towards Oxford in 1955. It is often stated that the Brunellian train shed at Banbury, which was built in 1850, survived until 1953, when it was replaced by a modern concrete and plate glass edifice. The building *did* survive until 1953, but it is often forgotten that only the train shed was then removed, and replaced by temporary canopies. The station was not completely rebuilt until 1958.

This 1955 view is of especial interest, therefore, in showing the transitional period. The extraordinary assembly of stock in the 'up' north bay is worthy of comment, as it includes a GWR toplight, an LNER lavatory coach, a GWR auto trailer and a goods brake van; truly a home for waifs and strays.

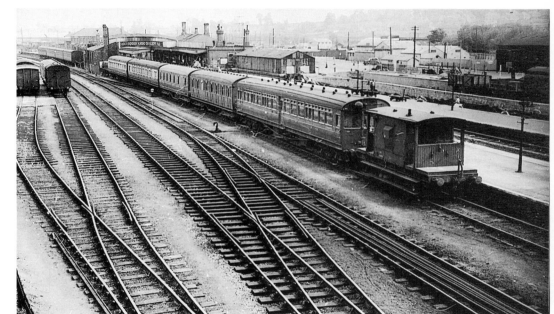

No. 6016 *King Edward V* approaches Banbury with a northbound express in 1952. In the last days of the Great Western and early BR years, the Birkenhead expresses via Bicester mostly called at Banbury, taking about 90 minutes from Paddington. Traditionally the first through service was about 9.10am ex-Paddington. In 1948, there were further services at 11.10am, 2.10pm, 4.10pm and 6.10pm, with various Wolverhampton, Aberystwyth and Shrewsbury services in between, providing an approximately hourly service as far as Wolverhampton in the main part of the day.

Above "Dean Goods" No. 2531, with the Banbury shed 'Loco Dept' vans, recalls the elegance of the Dean era. The locomotive dated from 1897, saw service in France in 1917-19, and was again requisitioned in 1940, and used on the Longmoor Military Railway, latterly for re-railing exercises, until 1959.

Below In 1930 Collett provided a successor to the "Dean Goods" the 2251 Class 0-6-0s. No. 3216, one of the last engines completed by the Great Western, in December 1947, commenced its career at Banbury, where it is seen five years later, with a class F unfitted freight.

Fenny Compton

Above The Oxford & Rugby, and Birmingham & Oxford Junction lines, which opened from Banbury to Birmingham in 1852, provided the Great Western with access to the West Midlands. The original intention was that the O&R should join the LNWR at Rugby, and the B&OJ join it north of Fenny Compton, but railway politics rendered the northern part of the O&R surplus, so that Fenny Compton was a minor wayside station until the coming of the independent East & West Junction Railway. The first section of this impecunious cross country route opened between Fenny Compton and Kineton in 1871. The GWR goods yard was thus sandwiched between the GWR main line – on the left – and the E&WJR, later Stratford-upon-Avon & Midland Junction Railway – on the right. No. 6970 *Whaddon Hall* heads a Leamington-bound express through Fenny Compton in 1955. The GWR platforms were staggered, the 'up' being on the left.

Below The 'up' buildings at Fenny Compton comprised a neat but small timber booking office and waiting room, plus the ubiquitous corrugated iron hut, the latter with the round roof accorded to sheds, rather than the pagoda granted to passengers. Such sheds were used as freight stores, for parcels, bicycles, station stores, and indeed any purpose the ingenuity of station staff could devise. In the left distance is a narrow level crossing, and next to it a road bridge. As the bridge was an advanced species of 'low bridge' the road user had the choice of the bridge, if his vehicle was small enough, or of annoying the signalman if it were not! The line in the foreground leads to the GWR goods yard and GWR/S&MJR freight interchange siding, for at this time there were no running connections.

Above Looking from the 'up' main to Banbury in 1964, with the 'up' refuge on the left, the 'up' platform in the distance, the BR 1960 signal cabin, and the down GWR platform. The BR box was part of an ambitious re-signalling scheme, providing running connections between the GW and SMJ for ironstone traffic between Banbury and South Wales.

Below No. 6833 *Calcot Grange* heads iron ore hoppers north along the GW main line on 27th July 1964. This scene, taken only a few feet from the photograph on the preceding page, shows the transformation as a result of the BR re-signalling.

Above Railway signal engineers were interesting people. On the Great Western (and on the North Eastern Railway), they obviously liked signals, and scattered them about enthusiastically. On the LNWR, they were less generous; probably they liked signals just as much, but the legacy of Richard Moon demanded economy. At Fenny Compton in 1960, the Western Region signal engineers had a field day in what was to be a very late mechanical re-signalling. BR Standard 2-6-4T No. 80072 is a curious choice of power for an iron ore train. It is in the 'down' reception loop, awaiting the passage of a Birmingham express, already signalled. Although only four years old, the interchange idea was doomed to imminent demise.

Below A double-chimney 'Castle', No. 5056 *Earl of Powis* heads a southbound holiday express along the triple track section between Greaves Sidings and Southam Road & Harbury station on 4th July 1964. The third line eased congestion in the 'down' direction, and is visible in the left foreground. No. 5056 had originally been an Old Oak engine, but finished its days at Oxley in November 1964. Her demise was a part of a batch of 'Castle' disposals from Oxley, with just a handful of engines lasting until the following February.

It is the early afternoon of 18th August 1956, and as a freight train waits in the 'up' refuge siding, No. 7010 *Avondale Castle* shatters the tranquillity of Southam Road & Harbury station as she roars through at the head of '183', the 'up' "Cambrian Coast Express".

Southam Road & Harbury

Above Southam Road & Harbury station, looking towards Banbury on 31st July 1964. As has been the case in so many places, nothing now remains of this pretty little country station, other than a pair of main line tracks.

Below No. 6011 *King James I* races northbound through Southam Road & Harbury station with just the least wisp of smoke from the double chimney, fitted in March 1956, just weeks before this evocative scene was recorded.

Above A carmine and cream BR delivery lorry is drawn up right by the entrance to the Italianate buildings at Harbury in July 1964. The fact that access to the buildings was virtually impossible hardly mattered, for no-one was likely to come, or so reasoned the staff! The Brunellian grace of the station is undermined by the flourishing crop of weeds sprouting from the gutters.

Below As a train is signalled in the 'down' direction, No. 2924 *Saint Helena* heads an 'up' parcels and stock train through Harbury during the summer of 1938 in an epitome of Great Western elegance.

Description of Train	REAR SECTION									Line	ADVANCE SECTION									Remarks and Delays
	IS LINE CLEAR				Train App-roach-ing Signal rec-eived	Train Enter-ing Section rec-eived	Train out of Section sent	Time Des-crip-tion Received	Train depart-ed or passed		IS LINE CLEAR				Train App-roach-ing Signal sent	Train Enter-ing Section sent	Train out of Section rec-eived	Time des-crip-tion sent	
	Rec-eived but not acc-epted	ACCEPTED									Offered but not acc-epted	ACCEPTED							
		under Reg. 5. See Note (a)	under Reg. 4A. See Note (b)	under Reg. 4 See Note (c)								under Reg. 5. See Note (a)	under Reg. 4A. See Note (b)	under Reg. 4. See Note (c)					
4 8/10 Padd				9.35	-42	-49								35		49	.55		
4 6.25. Padd				11.1	8	16								1		16	22		
				Monday October 22nd 1962															
1.3 1.7.10 Ken.				12.8	16	26								16		26	32		
2.3 Due				1.57	2.3	12								3		.12	20	Lydney
				Box visited 2.10 AM 'Deepdene' C.H.Marathon All in Order.															
1 4.4 125 Padd				2.48	55	3.9								48		33	9	-	
1.3 10.45 Padd 3.3				9	9	23		9.						20.		22.	29		
3.2 Reading				5.0	20	50								48 W.		48	6.6		
				R Abbow on Duty. Box															
				H. L. Hall On duty 6. an															
				Fosse Rd Switched in 6.14 an															
3.2 Old Oak.				7.1	8	13								.8		.13	.18	✓	
4 Didcot				8.36	44	47								.36		.47	.50		
4 6.55 Padd				9.18	24	25								.18		.25	.27		
4 8/20 Padd				9.59	10.4	5								.59		.5	.7		
				3.8.2 from Gravesend 10.13 brk 11.25															
4 9/0 Padd				10.16	.19	20								.16		.20	.22		
2.3 L.L.				10.22	.28	26								.22		.26	30		
4 9/10 Padd				10.34	.40	41								.34		.41	.43		
				Block Correct 11.0 an															
1.4 Wbury.				11.2	.7	.10								.2		.10	.14	✓	
4.1.3 Pullman				11.40	44	45								.40		.45	.47		
4 Oxford				12.0	.6	.7								.0		.7	.9		
1.4 11/30				12.21	24	26								.21		.26	.31		
4 1/0 Padd				1.5	.11	.13								.5		.13	.15		

Many enthusiasts will have seen the outside of a signal box, or in books upon railway mishaps, may have read of the train register, but with the steady demise of manual railway signalling, the chance to study a register is rare. We portray two pages from the Harbury register for 21st/22nd October 1962. Signal boxes were regularly visited by station masters or inspectors, but the 2.10am visit is in conjunction with a "Deepdene" move – a code word for a Royal Train, signalled as 4-4-4. Helpfully, the signalmen enter originating stations as well as bell codes in most cases.

Description of Train	REAR SECTION								Line	ADVANCE SECTION								Remarks and Delays
	IS LINE CLEAR				Train Approaching Signal received	Train Entering Section received	Train out of Section sent	Time Description Received	Train departed or passed		IS LINE CLEAR				Train Approaching Signal sent	Train Entering Section sent	Train out of Section received	Time description sent	
	Received but not accepted	ACCEPTED									Offered but not accepted	ACCEPTED							
		under Reg. 5. See Note (a)	under Reg. 4A. See Note (b)	under Reg. 4 See Note (c)								under Reg. 5. See Note (a)	under Reg. 4A. See Note (b)	under Reg. 4. See Note (c)					
4 7/5 Wh'ptk				8·52	4·3	·11								·3	·11	20		
							Labour on Duty 10·0pm											
							7 A Hands off duty 10·0pm											
4 3·13 Abbey Sg'ls				10·30	·41	50								·41	50	11·1	*No R8 1 S*	
							Monday· October 22nd 1962											
4 12·15 Bham				12·30	·43	50								·43	50	·59	·100	1·S —
4 9·55 B'head				1·30	·52	53								·52	53	55		·1
3·1 1·10 Wolv'tn				·53	53	2·7								2·5	·7	26		·1
1·4 Wolv'tn				·41	16	32								16	32	5·11		
2·3 Due				·51	57	20								·11	20	33		
							Greave Leamy Compton opened 5·30am											
3·2 3·12 W Sh'n				5·48	50	6·11								50	·11	·28		
3·2 Bilston				6·11	·11	·35			·28					·33	·33	·46		
3·1 6·50 Leam				6·53	7·0	·4								·0	·4	·10		
3·2 S'n Wheaton				7·4	·4	·10								·10	·14	·16		
							Greave Sg'ls Switched in 7·9											
4 1·3 Pullman				8·6	·10	·13								·10	·13	·14		1·S
4 Wh'mp				8·29	·36	·39								·36	·39	·41		1·6
4 Tree				8·39	·41	·44								·41	·44	·45		1·5
4 Salop				8·59	9·3	·6								·3	·6	·7		1·5
3·2 Bromb'o				9·10	·15	·26								·15	·23	·28		Coupled
4 Salop				9·21	·36	·38								·36	·38	·40		1·5
2·3 L.C.				9·38	·38	·42								·40	·42	·47		
4 Wh'mp				9·52	·57	·59								·57	·59	10·0		
3·14 Ballast				9·59	·59	10·6								·0	5·	·8		
3 Local											10·8				·8	·16		
4 B'head				10·33	·38	·41								·38	·41	·42		1·5
3·2 Wheat'n				10·57	11·7	·13								·7	·13	·15		
4 B'head				11·30	·34	·37								·34	·37	·38		1·6
4 Margate				11·50	·55	·58								·55	·58	·59		
4 B'head				12·30	·34	·37								·34	·37	·38		1·5
3·1·1				12·37	37	·42								·38	·42	·43		
2·3 L.C.				12·44	·44	·50								·44	·50	·52		
4 B'mouth				1·11	·18	·21								·18	·21	·22		
2·3 L.C.				1·21	·22	·25								·22	·25	·28		

45

Opposite top From Southam Road & Harbury station the line is on a continuous falling grade for the six miles to Leamington Spa, which is situated in a hollow. This was inconvenient enough for the railway surveyors, but even worse, a ridge of higher ground intervenes just west of Harbury. Instead of climbing to avoid this higher terrain, the line had to fall at 1 in 187 for some three miles, and this led to one of the principal earthworks on the Birmingham line. From its commencement, *east* of Harbury station, which is in a shallow cutting, to its western limits is over two miles, but the daunting section is about a mile west of the station, where it reaches a depth of 110 feet. As the material was fairly treacherous, and there was a bad slip during construction in 1850, a very gentle angle of repose was necessary. The cutting culminates in the 73 yard long Harbury Tunnel, which would have been longer, had it not been for the slip. Quarter of a mile west of the tunnel, a higher overbridge provides access to Bull Ring Farm, and it is from this bridge that the next two plates were taken in 1956. In this illustration, looking east from Bull Ring Farm bridge towards Harbury, we see 2-8-0 No. 2867 drifting down hill with a long class F ironstone train. In the far distance, beyond the brake, we can see the enormous brick curved wing wall and retaining wall of Harbury tunnel.

Opposite below The view to the west is even more dramatic, for as No. 2867 and train wind their way towards the end of the cutting at Westfields, No. 6927 *Lilford Hall* erupts into volcanic action as she struggles to keep a heavy mineral train moving up the hill to Harbury summit. Her exhaust stretches sixty or seventy feet into the sky, but even more dramatic than this is the way in which engine and train are dwarfed into insignificance by the setting. If any two views in this book had to be singled out to epitomise the Birmingham line, it would be these two. 'Halls' and '28xxs' hammering their way up hill, and drifting down grade with a string of freights, coal, ironstone, limestone, cars, castings, produce and general goods.

Above This 1938 portrait of No. 5921 *Bingley Hall,* in charge of a seven coach express near Leamington, recalls all the elegance of the Great Western. The train appears to comprise a four coach rake with two additional vehicles at the front, one a 9-compartment *'Toplight',* and one at the rear. At this time, the GWR was still painting its carriage roofs white, but modellers should study this rake; smoke grey is the shade they rapidly assumed in service.

Whitnash Cutting

Above No. 5063 entered service as *Thornbury Castle* in June 1937, but the controversy over 'Earl' names for the rather old-fashioned 'Dukedog' 4-4-0s, led to a rethink. The 'Earl' names were switched to the newest 'Castles', beginning with Nos 5052 and 5063, the latter becoming *Earl Baldwin*. She is on the 'up' express south of Leamington in 1938, a most peculiar turn for a locomotive which was the pride and joy of Worcester shed! This was the last 'Earl' to succumb, lasting until February 1965. When the authors last saw No. 5063, at Gloucester shed upon her demise, grimy and shorn of plates, it was a sad contrast to the immaculate engine seen here.

Below An 'Aberdare', 2-6-0 No. 2656, plods north with a lowly class H 'mineral or ballast train' near Leamington Spa in 1938. She has acquired an ROD tender, but mercifully, has retained the tall safety valve bonnet, rather than the squashed variety inflicted on a number of 'Aberdares'. These engines, with their blend of Dean and Churchward ideas, symbolise the transformation which took place at Swindon at the turn of the century. It is sad that such a fascinating link between the Victorian and 'Modern' Great Western did not last into the preservation era, but the last 'Aberdares' went in 1949, and had it not been for the War, they would have gone sooner.

Above As the day draws on, No. 6005 *King George II* storms up through Whitnash cutting on the 1 in 202 climb which starts just outside Leamington Spa, and which after easing briefly, sharpens to a gruelling three miles of 1 in 187 to Harbury. It is the summer of 1939, and events in Europe are casting shadows quite different to those laid down by No. 6005.

Below A war had come, and gone, a new government had decreed the death knell of the Great Western Railway, but the challenge remains the same. '56xx', 6697 blasts her way up Whitnash bank with a class K trip freight in August 1948. No. 6697 was the last 5600 class 0-6-2T in BR service, lasting until May 1966, and is now, happily, preserved at the Didcot Railway Centre. Of the standard gauge GWR stud, just a handful of pannier tanks outlasted her, and these only by a few months.

Leamington Spa

Above As the sun sinks slowly, a 'curved frame 72xx', No. 7207, climbs the 1 in 202 bank out of Leamington Spa towards Harbury. In the left distance is the GWR loco shed, which replaced an earlier shed in 1906. It housed some thirty engines, almost half of which were customarily 2-6-2Ts for the suburban services, pilot duties and some freight work. There was usually a brood of '56xx' 0-6-2Ts for trip freight, three or four 4-6-0s for semi-fasts, and a smattering of panniers. The second and third wagons in the train are examples of the curious canvas-sided BoCar wagons, introduced to carry motor car bodies – indeed the sheets on the leading 'BoCar' speak of 'MOTOR CAR BODIES & PRESSINGS FROM THE PRESSED STEEL CO OXFORD'.

Opposite right 'Leamington Spa South Junction Signal Box' in August 1965. This was a perfect example of the new standard signal box introduced about 1900. Although these boxes were frequently built by outside contractors, uniformity was obtained by the highly detailed specifications, and by the Great Western supplying not only the special items, such as roof vents, but the bricks as well. Specifications were provided for the ancillary items too, such as the coal and ash bin in the foreground, complete even to the half round coping. The box was built to control access to the 1906 loco shed, the coal stage/water tank of which is seen on the extreme right, and a new connection to the LNWR (which runs adjacent to the GWR). The new connection, which was opened on 10th July 1908, diverged from the LNWR near the sheds, and the splitting home signals are visible just to the right of the box. It joined the GWR just beyond the signal cabin, out of the picture. A through service was provided between Cardiff and Yarmouth in 1908-09, but failed to prosper, nor did the connection carry much traffic.

Opposite below A signalman's world! In studying the signal diagram, we see the connection to the shed and coach sidings to the left of the box, but that the connections to the LNWR have been deleted. On the block shelf are two late period Reading block instruments, each with separate bell, the near one tall and coned, the far one flat, to give different tones.

Above Leamington Spa, with its classical Regency architecture, was the only sizeable community between Banbury and Birmingham, and as befitted its Spa status, and affluent clientele, received a Brunellian timber train shed when the line opened in 1852. Not only was it much longer than the 1850 roof at Banbury, but it spanned four tracks, rather than two. Smoke extraction must have been a major problem, and the corrosive effects of locomotive exhausts could not have been good for timber or ironwork. The shed was cut back to level with the platform edges, but as the roof then gave negligible protection to passengers, it was further cut back to the line of the columns between 1905 and 1911, and a utilitarian screen added, sloping downwards towards the rails. We are looking towards Banbury c1933.

Below No. 7315, a 4300 class 2-6-0, enters Leamington station with an 'up' express in the early thirties. Assuming the station was similar to those at Weymouth and Merthyr Tydfil, which were of similar span and vintage, the space behind the 'X' beams would have originally been open, with the sloping roof beams supported from the lower horizontal beam by curved timbers. The public footbridge, from which the previous view was taken, is visible in the distance. The first two carriages are of particular interest as they are two of the three diagram G.54 Third class private saloons (Nos 9364-9366) built in 1920 on older chassis. They appear to have 'Reserved' notices in the windows, so doubtless have been hired by a private party. Great Western timetables of the day noted that private saloons and family carriages, invalid carriages and saloons for parties were available upon timely application to the Superintendent of the Line.

Above Leamington shed customarily boasted a number of passenger engines, usually handed down from more important sheds, for its semi-fast turns. No. 3711 *City of Birmingham,* had once been a top link express engine, but was eking out her last days prior to withdrawal in July 1930, when captured on a semi-fast working. Of the 93 large wheeled 6ft 8½in Dean double frame 4-4-0s in service in 1927, not one remained by 1932, due to the flood of new 4-6-0s emerging from Swindon. Note the old red-painted headlamp.

Below After the purge of the large-wheeled Dean 4-4-0s, Leamington graduated on to 'Saints', but after the War, acquired a relatively modern passenger engine for a change, in the shape of the 1938-built No. 7810 *Draycott Manor.* It is depicted entering the 'down' platform in October 1947. The grimy and travel-stained condition is a reflection of wartime and early post-war shortages of staff, from which even the Great Western was not immune. It is quite a contrast to the smart turnout of No. 3711 in the previous plate.

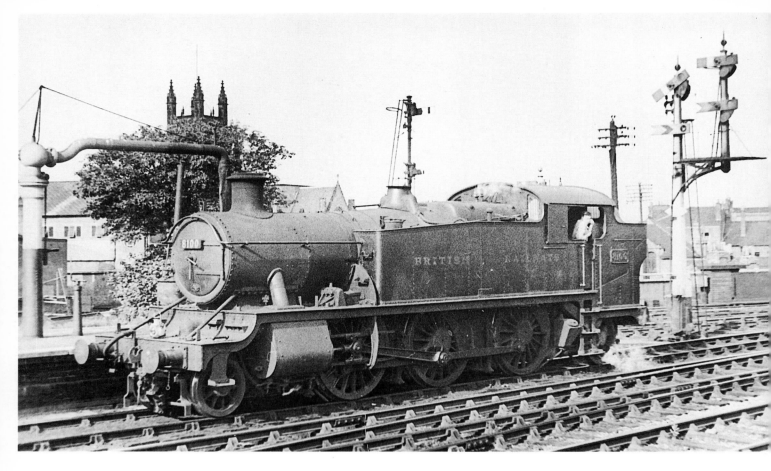

Above Leamington was also home for the original Churchward large Prairie, in its later guise as No. 8100. She was built in 1903 as No. 99 in the "prototype" number series, renumbered 3100 in 1912, 5100 in 1929, and the frames used with new curved front ends to produce the first of the 8100 class in 1938. Fifty were scheduled to be rebuilt, but only ten were completed before war curtailed the project. It is seen at Leamington in early BR livery with GWR-style 'BRITISH RAILWAYS' lettering in 1951. She ended her days, still at Leamington, in 1962.

Below Leamington also looked after two or three of the GWR diesel railcars for many years. No. 26 was built in 1940, though stored until March 1942. By 1947 she was at Leamington, and became No. W26 under British Railways in which guise she is seen in 1952. The GWR cars operated a number of the Stratford services, and one of the authors, even as a child, realised intuitively that these stylish cars in their red and cream were infinitely superior to the boring dmus which BR insisted on producing.

Above Leamington was the outer terminus of the Birmingham suburban services, and a Tyseley-based 5101 class Prairie, No. 4116, has arrived in the 'up' platform with a morning train in 1950. She is in BR lined passenger black with the early 'lion and wheel' emblem.

Below Today, 'Inter-City' applies to BR's principal express services, but in the fifties it had a more specific meaning. It was the 8.20am from Paddington to Birmingham, Wolverhampton, Shrewsbury and Chester, and its return working, at 2.30pm from Chester. No. 5010 *Restormel Castle* calls at Leamington with the 'up' train in 1951.

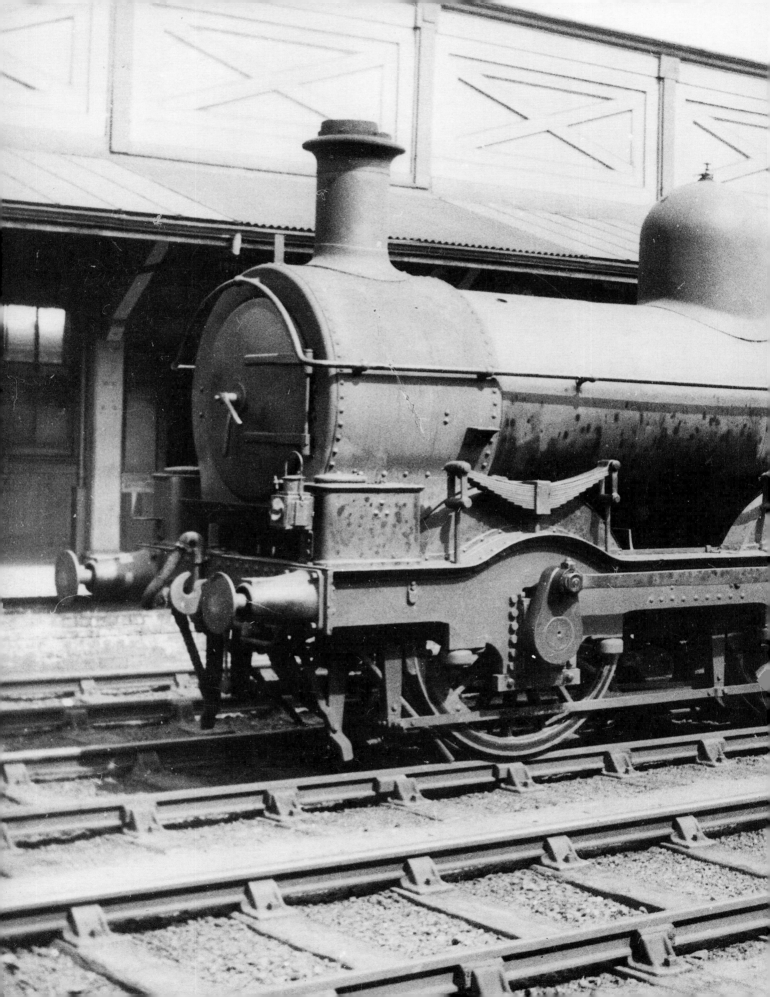

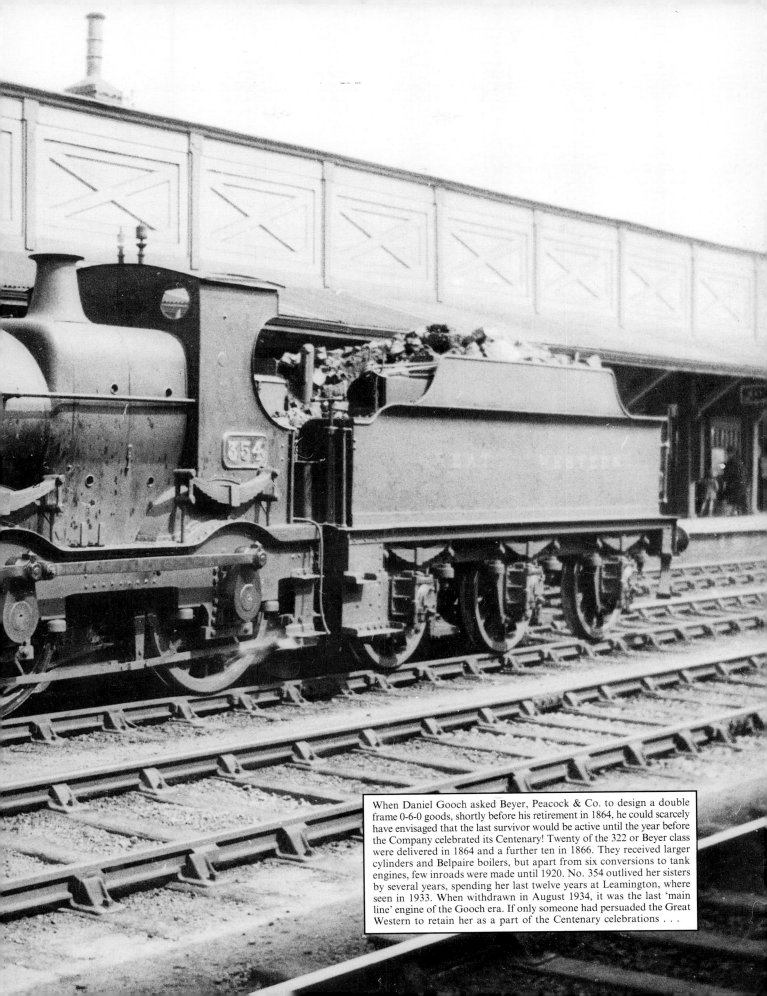

When Daniel Gooch asked Beyer, Peacock & Co. to design a double frame 0-6-0 goods, shortly before his retirement in 1864, he could scarcely have envisaged that the last survivor would be active until the year before the Company celebrated its Centenary! Twenty of the 322 or Beyer class were delivered in 1864 and a further ten in 1866. They received larger cylinders and Belpaire boilers, but apart from six conversions to tank engines, few inroads were made until 1920. No. 354 outlived her sisters by several years, spending her last twelve years at Leamington, where seen in 1933. When withdrawn in August 1934, it was the last 'main line' engine of the Gooch era. If only someone had persuaded the Great Western to retain her as a part of the Centenary celebrations . . .

For Local Tables, see pages	Down Trains.		Week Days.																		
			a.m.	n'gt	a.m.	a.m.	a.m.	a.m.	a.m.	a.m.	a.m.	a.m.	a.m.	a.m.	a.m.	a.m.	a.m.	a.m.	a.m.	a.m.
	LONDON (Paddington) dep			12 15																	
	Ealing (Broadway)																				
75, 76	Bournemouth (Central) dep			7 11																	
	Portsmouth Town "			6 58																	
	Southampton Docks "			8 2																	
	Basingstoke "			9 12																	
	Reading dep			1 16																	
	Didcot arr																				
	Bristol (Temple Meads) dep																				
	Weymouth "																				
	Swindon "																				
	Didcot dep																				
	Culham "																				
	Radley "																				
153	Abingdon { arr / dep																				
	OXFORD { arr / dep			1 54 / 2 2																	
158	Wolvercot Halt "																				
	Kidlington (for Blenheim) "																				
	Bletchington "																				
	Heyford "																				
	Fritwell and Somerton "																				
	Aynho for Deddington "																				
64 to 69 / 103, 142	King's Sutton "																				
	Banbury "			2 35																	
	Cropredy "																				
	Fenny Compton "																				
	Southam Road and Harbury "																				
	Leamington { arr / dep			3 8 / 3 12																	
	Warwick "											7 25										
	Hatton arr											7 30										
150 to 153	Stratford-on-Avon { arr / dep											7 39										
											8 54										
	Hatton dep											7 15										
153	Lapworth "											7 42										
	Knowle and Dorridge "									6 5	7 0	7 52			8 2							
	Widney Manor "											7 59			8 8	8 15				8 31		
	Solihull "								6 12	7 9	7 35	7 45			8 12	8 17	8 25	8 34	8 39		
	Olton "								6 17	7 14	7 40	7 50			8 17	8 22	8 30	8 39	8 45		
	Acock's Green and South Yardley "								6 20	7 17	7 43	7 53			8 20	8 25	8 33	8 43	8 49		
	Tyseley "								6 23	7 16	7 46	7 56				8 28	8 37		8 52		
	Small Heath and Sparkbrook "					5 25		6 10	6 26	7 23	7 50	7 59			8 25	8 31	8 40		8 55		
	Bordesley "					5 28		6 15	6 29	7 27	7 54	8 4	8 14	8 30		8 35	8 45	8 52	8 58		
148 to 159	**BIRMINGHAM** { Moor Street arr				5 34		6 20	6 32	7 32	8 0	8 9	8 20			8 40		8 55			
	{ Snow Hill { arr / dep		3 48 / 3 53	STOP		6 0	6 35	STOP	7 50	8 0	STOP	8 30	8 38	STOP		8 50	STOP	9 5		
	Hockley "					6 4	6 39		7 54				8 42							
	Soho and Winson Green "					6 10	6 42		7 57				8 45							
	Handsworth and Smethwick "					6 16	6 46		8 2			8 40	8 50							
	West Bromwich "					6 20	6 52		8 8				8 57							
	Swan Village "					6 25	6 56		8 12				9 1							
	Wednesbury "						7 1		8 16				9 7							
	Bradley and Moxley "					6 31			8 20				9 11							
	Bilston "					6 35	7 7		8 25				9 16							
	Priestfield "					6 39	7 11		8 30				9 20							
	WOLVERHAMPTON { arr / dep (Low Level)		4 17 / 4 22			6 39 / 6 43	7 15 / 7 10	STOP	7 25	8 35			8 56 / 9 0	9 25						
	Dunstall Park "								7 26											
	Codsall "						R	7 20												
	Albrighton "						R	7 27	7 42											
	Shifnal "						7 2	STOP	7 51				9 19							
	Oakengates "						7 12		8 0	a.m.		a.m.	9 30							
	Wellington "		2 46		7 10		7 24		8 7	8 17		9 33	9 45							
164	**Crewe**						8 50	STOP				10 55								
	MANCHESTER (London Rd.)						10 0					12 24								
	Admaston dep					7 15			8 22											
	Walcot "					7 20			8 28											
	Upton Magna "					7 27			8 34											
	Shrewsbury arr		3 0 / 5 5		7 35	7 43			8 45		9 47	10 0								
166	Welshpool arr				STOP	8 45						11 5							
	Aberystwyth					11 40						2 15								
	Shrewsbury dep		5 15	6 30		8 0			8 0			10 5								
	Leaton "								8 9											
	Baschurch "			6 45		8 16			8 16			10 19								
	Rednal and West Felton "			6 56	M	8 27			8 27				M							
	Whittington "			7 2	a.m.	8 36			8 36				a.m.							
	Gobowen "			7 10	8 7	8 45			8 45			10 37	11 13							
138	**Oswestry** { arr / dep			7 17 / 6 58		8 55 / 8 0			8 55 / 8 35			10 47 / 10 15	11 6							
	Preesgweene (for Weston Rhyn) dep			7 15		8 49			8 49			10 44	11 18							
	Chirk "			7 19		8 16			8 56				11 22							
	Whitehurst Halt "					8 20							11 26							
	Cefn "			7 25		8 24	9 2						11 30	M						
	Rhosymedre Halt "				a.m.	8 27		a.m.					11 33	a.m.						
	Ruabon "			7 35	8 25	8 30	9 9	9 2		a.m.	10 3		10 55	11 35	11 45					
167	Dolgelley arr			9 40				11 40						1 5						
	Barmouth			10 10				12 12						1 42						
	Johnstown and Hafod dep			7 40	8 28		9 6	a.m.							11 49					
	Wrexham "		5 58	7 47	8 37	9 17	9 21	9 25	10 11			11 3			11 57					
	Gresford "			7 58	8 45			9 32							12 6					
	Rossett "			8 1	8 50			9 35							12 11					
	Balderton "			8 13				9 45							12 17					
	Saltney "			8 21											12 22					
	Chester arr		6 20	8 32	9 1			9 55	10 35			11 30			12 28					
170 {	Birkenhead (Woodside) arr		7 5	9 6	9 32		10 7	10 46	11 6				11 50			1 16				
	LIVERPOOL { Landing Stage { Central (L. Level)		7 25 / 7 18	9 20 / 9 14	9 50 / 9 33		10 20 / 10 18	10 50 / 10 50	11 6 / 11 14				12 10 / 12 2			1 30 / 1 22				
172	Warrington arr		8 15	9 16	10 23			10 37	11 27				12 13							
	Manchester (Exchange) "		9 10	9 56				11 20					1 0							

M—Rail Motor Car; one class only.
O—Calls at Ruabon to set down Passengers from London on notice being given by the Passenger to the Guard at Shrewsbury.
P—Calls at Culham to pick up Passengers for Banbury and beyond on notice being given at the Station.
R—Calls at Codsall and Albrighton to pick up Passengers for Stations beyond Wellington, on notice being given at the Station.

On Bank Holidays several Trains shewn in this table will not run, and others will run at altered times. **See Special Announcement.**

NOTE:—For **COMPLETE SERVICES** between — see pages
TYSELEY AND BIRMINGHAM 148–149
STRATFORD-ON-AVON AND BIRMINGHAM .. 150–151
BIRMINGHAM AND WOLVERHAMPTON 154–155
BIRMINGHAM AND DUDLEY 156–157
BIRMINGHAM AND STOURBRIDGE JUNCTION 158–159

NEW ROUTE LONDON (Paddington), **BIRMINGHAM, SHREWSBURY, NORTH WALES, CHESTER, AND BIRKENHEAD** Via BICESTER.

Through Train to Worcester, Newport & Cardiff.

Down Trains.		Week Days.																		
		a.m.	a.m.	a.m.	a.m.	a.m.	a.m.	a.m.	a.m.	a.m.	a.m.	a.m.	a.m.	a.m.	a.m.	a.m.	a.m.	a.m.	a.m.	p.m.
LONDON { Paddington	dep	5 30					5 45	5 40		6 30		6 55		7 30			8 48	9 10	
{ Victoria (S.E.&C.&G.W.)	,,																	8 15	
Ealing (Broadway)							5 59			6 8			7 40			8 35			
Bournemouth (Central)	dep													6 10				
Portsmouth Town	,,													6 45	6§37	7§39			
Southampton Docks	,,													8 5				
Basingstoke	,,																	
Reading	dep		6 18					6 40		7 44			8 38		9 21	9§10	9§43		
Didcot	arr		6 40					7 3		8 0			STOP			7 45		9 40	
Bristol (Temple Meads)	dep		3 45												9 0			
Weymouth	,,									6 30								
Swindon	,,		4 55															
Didcot	dep		6 50					7 20		8 10			9 34	9 50				
Culham	,,							7 27		P			9 41					
Radley	,,							7 35		8 27			9 48					
Abingdon { arr								7 50		8 37			10 3					
{ dep								7 5		7 59			9 30					
OXFORD { arr			7 5					7 44	M	8 36		9 5	M	9 57	10 5	10 15		
{ dep	,,		7 12					7 50	8 12	8 42	9 0	STOP	9 30			10 20		
Wolvercot Halt	,,								8 18				9 39					
Kidlington (for Blenheim)	,,								8 5	8 27		U					
Bletchington	,,								8 11	8 32							
Heyford	,,								8 20	8 44							
Fritwell and Somerton	,,							M	8 27		M					
Aynho for Deddington	,,							8V17	8 33				a.m.			
King's Sutton	,,							8 24	8 39	8 50			10 34			
Banbury	,,		7 42			8 10		8 32	8 50	8 57	9 17	9 35	10 41	10 50		
Cropredy	,,		STOP			8 19		8 59					STOP		
Fenny Compton	,,					8 28		STOP	9 10						
Southam Road and Harbury	,,					8 37			9 20						
Leamington	dep		8 25		9 0	8 45		9 30	9 37	9 45	9 50	10 15			
Warwick			8 31		9 5		9 42	9 56	10 20				
Hatton	arr		8 40		9 34		9 51	10 6	10 28				
Stratford-on-Avon { arr			8 30		9 20			9 45	10 50			
{ dep												
Hatton	dep		8 41		9 36		9 53	10 10				
Lapworth	,,		8 49		9 23		a.m.	10 2				
Knowle and Dorridge	,,		8 55		9 30		9 50	10 9				
Widney Manor	,,						9 55				
Solihull	,,			9 8	9 15	9 37		9 59	10 16			
Olton	,,			9 20			10 4	10 19			
Acock's Green and South Yardley	,,			9 23			10 8	10 25			
Tyseley	,,			9 26			10 11	10 30			
Small Heath and Sparkbrook	,,			9 29			10 15	10 34			
Bordesley	,,		9 9	9 17	9 34	9 46	9 55	10 19	10 38		
BIRMINGHAM { Moor St. arr			9 14	9 22	9 40	9 52	9 58	10 3				
{ Snow Hill dep		9 10	9 14	9 30	9 40	9 52		10 24	10 45	10 34	10 43	11 10	
Hockley	,,		STOP	9 30	STOP	10 0		10 40	10 47	11 15	
Soho and Winson Green	,,							10 50		
Handsworth and Smethwick	,,			9 36		10 10		10 54		
West Bromwich	,,			9 43		10 15		10 59		
Swan Village	,,					10 19		11 4		
Wednesbury	,,			9 53		10 24		11 8		
Bradley and Moxley	,,					10 28		11 11		
Bilston	,,			10 3		10 32		11 14		
Priestfield	,,					10 36		11 18		
WOLVERHAMPTON { arr		9 30		10 9		10 40		11 0	11 23	11 34	
(Low Level) { dep		9 35		10 15				11 15		11 39	
Dunstall Park	,,			10 18					
Codsall	,,			10 27					
Albrighton	,,			10 37					
Shifnal	,,			10 48					
Oakengates	,,			a.m. 10 58					
Wellington	,,		11 3	11 10				11 47		W
Crewe	arr							1 0		
MANCHESTER (London Rd.)	,,							1 55		
Admaston	dep			11 15					
Walcot	,,			11 22					
Upton Magna	,,			11 30					
Shrewsbury	arr	10 13		11 17	11 45				12 17
Welshpool	arr	11 5							
Aberystwyth	,,	2 15 a.m.							
Shrewsbury	dep		11 20						12 20
Leaton	,,		11 28						
Baschurch	,,		11 36						
Rednal and West Felton	,,		11 47						
Whittington	,,		11 54						
Gobowen	,,		12 1						
Oswestry { arr			12 10						
{ dep			11 43						
Preesgweene (for Weston Rhyn)	dep		12 6						
Chirk	,,		12 10						
Whitehurst Halt	,,								
Cefn	,,		12 16						
Rhosymedre Halt	,,				p.m.				
Ruabon	,,		12 23		12 35				
Dolgelley	arr								
Barmouth									
Johnstown and Hafod	dep		12 27						
Wrexham	,,		12 35		12 43				1 3	1 8
Gresford	,,								1 15
Rossett	,,								1 19
Balderton	,,								1 24
Saltney	,,								1 33
Chester	arr				1 5			1 23	1 42
Birkenhead (Woodside)	arr				1 57			1 57	2 31
LIVERPOOL { Landing Stage					2 10			2 10	2 50
{ Central (L Level)					2 2			2 2	2 42
Warrington	arr				1 50				2 28
Manchester (Exchange)	,,				2 20				3 7

NEW EXPRESS
CONTINENTAL SERVICE.

Bale (Central)	dep	10.14 a.m.
Munich	,,	9. 0 ,,
Dresden	,,	8. 8 ,,
Leipsic	,,	10.26 ,,
Frankfurt-on-the-Maine	,,	2.56 p.m.
Cologne	,,	7.10 ,,
Berlin	,,	11.40 a.m.
Hanover	,,	3.36 p.m.
Hamburg	,,	2 44 ,,
Bremen	,,	4.26 ,,
Antwerp	,,	8.21 ,,
Amsterdam	,,	8.20 ,,
The Hague	,,	8.57 ,,
Rotterdam	,,	9.47 ,,
Flushing	,,	12.10 a.m.
Folkestone	,,	6. 0 ,,
Victoria (SE & C & GW)	arr.	7.47 ,,
Paris (St. Lazare)	dep	9 20 p.m.
Newhaven Harbour	,,	6 0 a.m.
Victoria (L.B. & S.C.)	arr.	7 30 ,,
Victoria (SE & C & GW)	dep.	8 15 a.m.
Leamington	arr.	10 44 ,,
Birmingham	,,	11 10 ,,
Wolverhampton	,,	11 34 ,,

For full particulars see pages iv & v.

U—Calls at Bletchington and Heyford to pick up Passengers for the Great Central Line, on notice being given at the Station.
V—Aynho Park platform.
W—Carriage slipped at Wellington at 12.3 p.m.
§—Via Newbury.
*—Slip Carriage.
+—Wrexham arrive 9.12 a.m. ‡—Southampton West.
¶—July 21st to September 16th only.

THURSDAYS EXCEPTED. / To Great Central Line. / Via Beaconsfield. / THURSDAYS ONLY. / Birmingham, Chester & Birkenhead Express, (Via Bicester. Breakfast Car Train. / To Great Central Line. / Carriage slipped at Leamington at 10.44 a.m. / Luncheon Car Train. / Through Carriage from Folkestone to Birmingham and Wolverhampton, in connection with Continental Service via Flushing. / Via Bicester. / JULY 14th, 16th AND DAILY JULY 21st to SEPTEMBER 16th.

For Complete Service between Tyseley, Birmingham and Swan Village, see pages 148 and 154.

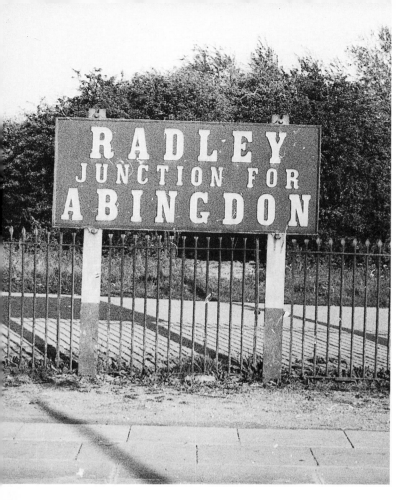

Branch Lines – The South

Radiating from the Birmingham line were a number of branches, each with their own character and charm. In this portrait of the Great Western from Paddington to the Mersey, it would be a pity to ignore the little branch trains simmering in the bay platforms, which were once such a feature of main line travel.

Radley

Left The GWR was above all things, a 'thoughtful' railway; bullnose bricks on buildings avoided sharp corners; big signs at stations made for clarity. Sadly, design consultants of today prefer fashion to such commonsense.

Below We commence our voyage into the byways with one of those delightful little Collett 0-4-2Ts, No. 1437, on a single auto coach at Radley, junction for Abingdon. The branch opened in 1856, but it was not until 1873, when connections with the main line were altered, that Radley station came into being. The branch was 2½ miles long with a ruling grade of 1 in 200 falling to Abingdon. Under the GWR 'Route Colour' system, it was uncoloured, and was restricted to '48xx' (later '14xx') and '58xx' tanks. The line closed to passengers in September 1963, a decade after this scene was recorded.

RADLEY AND ABINGDON. (Third class only.)

		a.m.	a.m.	a.m.		a.m.	a.m.		p.m.	p.m.		p.m.	p.m.	p.m.	p.m.		p.m.	p.m.	p.m.		Sundays p.m.	p.m.	p.m.
Radley	dep.	7 25	8 20	9 10	...	10 15	11 10	...	1 50	2 35	...	3 57	5 10	5 38	6 40	...	7 7	8 55	9 50	...	7 35	9 9	10 25
Abingdon	arr.	7 35	8 25	9 15	.	10 20	11 15	.	1 55	2 40	.	4 2	5 15	5 43	6 45	.	7 12	9 0	9 55	.	7 40	9 14	10 30

		a.m.	a.m.	a.m.		a.m.	a.m.		p.m.	p.m.		p.m.	p.m.	p.m.	p.m.		p.m.	p.m.	p.m.		p.m.	p.m.	p.m.
Abingdon	dep.	7 2	8 5	8 38	...	9 55	10 52	...	1 22	2 22	...	3 42	4 52	5 25	6 20	...	6 50	8 30	9 35	...	7 20	8 52	10 5
Radley	arr.	7 12	8 10	8 43	...	10 0	10 57	..	1 27	2 27	.	3 47	4 57	5 30	6 25	.	6 55	8 35	9 40	...	7 25	8 57	10 10

KIDLINGTON AND BLENHEIM AND WOODSTOCK.
Week Days only. (Third class only.)

		T a.m.	a.m.	a.m.	p.m.	S p.m.	Q p.m.	T p.m.	Y p.m.	p.m.
Kidlington dep.		7 20	8 40	11 15	12 38	12 58	2 35	4 10	5 38	6 42
Shipton-on-Cherwell † „		7 26	8 46	11 20	12 43	1 3	2 40	4 15	5 43	6 47
Blenheim and Woodstock arr.		7 30	8 50	11 23	12 46	1 6	2 43	4 18	5 46	6 50

		a m	a m	p.m.	p.m.	S p.m.	G p.m.	T p.m.	S p.m.	G p.m.	T p.m.	p.m.
Blenheim and Woodstock dep.		7 58	9 25	12 22	12 42	12 58	1 18	3 52	5 22	6 20	7 0	
Shipton-on-Cherwell † „		8 1	9 28	12 25	12 45	1 1	1 21	3 55	5 25	6 23	7 3	
Kidlington arr.		8 6	9 33	12 30	12 50	1 6	1 26	4 0	5 30	6 28	7 8	

G—Saturdays excepted.
J—Wrexham arrive 9.13 a.m.
K—Calls at Wellington at 5.15 a.m. and Gobowen 6.23 a.m. to set down passengers only.
L—Mondays only.
N—Calls during daylight only.
P—Wellington arrive 7.6 a.m.
Q—Calls at 4.57 a.m. to set down passengers on notice being given by the passenger to the Guard at Wolverhampton.
S—Saturdays only.

T—Through service between Oxford and Blenheim & Woodstock.
X—Third class only (limited accommodation).
Y—On Saturdays, through train from Oxford (depart 4.0 p.m.).
†—Halt.
§—Gobowen arrive 11.25 a.m.
③—Third class only.

Above The Great Western timetables for 22nd May 1944 reveal quite an intensive service on the Abingdon branch between 7am and 10pm, and also include the rather lighter service on the Blenheim branch north of Oxford. Some of the notes relate to other services for which we do not have room on this page.

Right Despite the high degree of standardisation applied in so many fields, Great Western station signs shewed a pleasing diversity right into BR days. In comparing the Abingdon and Radley signs, the posts differ in type, position and painting, the proportions and edging of the board differs, the letters differ. Indeed there is precious little that is the same!

Below Abingdon station looked towards Radley in 1953, with the malt house sidings to the left, then the signal box, water tank and loco shed to the right of the running lines. A steam roller stands at the top of the goods yard.

Kidlington

Above To the pioneer 'enthusiasts' the Woodstock branch's principal claim to fame was its regular locomotive, No. 1473 *Fair Rosamund.* No. 1473 began life as a perfectly ordinary member of the Wolverhampton built 517 class 0-4-2Ts. The earliest were saddle tanks, but later were altered to side tanks in common with newer examples. They were intended for local passenger duties and branch lines, but with the increasing weight of suburban trains, eventually gravitated to auto work on the branches or as shunters. No. 1473 was a late example of the class, being built in 1883. In 1896, she was selected to haul a Royal Train conveying Queen Victoria, and for reasons which defy logical explanation, the Great Western felt it would be a nice idea to name the engine *Fair Rosamund.* Except for one small detail, this was all very splendid; the detail was that the original Rosamund was a ward of King Henry II, whom the king set up as his mistress in a lovenest near Woodstock! The frequent visits did not go down too well with his queen, the strong-willed Eleanor of Aquitaine, whose own visit to Woodstock resulted in Rosamund's precipitate demise! The Great Western *Fair Rosamund* fared rather better; she is seen at Kidlington on 20th October 1930, and survived until August 1935.

Blenheim & Woodstock

Left Possibly the most celebrated Great Western branch of all was the $3\frac{3}{4}$ mile line from Kidlington just north of Oxford to Blenheim & Woodstock. The line was built by the independent Woodstock Railway, with the financial backing of the Duke of Marlborough, and opened on 19th March, 1890. It was taken over by the GWR shortly thereafter. To most railways, the terminus would have been Woodstock, or 'Woodstock for Blenheim', but given the antecedents of the branch and the Great Western's *patrician* leanings, it was only natural that the Palace of Blenheim would take precedence over the village!

Despite its pedigree, traffic was not heavy, and the line closed to all traffic in March 1954, long before the Beeching era. In 1951, the station sign was in flawless condition, as was the graceful lamp standard adjacent to it. When we look at this sign, and see how clearly it imparts the necessary information, one must ask why road and rail 'designers' of today opt for lower case lettering which is so much harder to decipher from a moving vehicle, particularly at an angle or in poor light.

Above Over the last two decades of its life, the branch saw a variety of Collett '48xx' 0-4-2Ts, the 1930's successors to the old 517 class, but none achieved the immortality of *Fair Rosamund.* A Collett tank, with an auto coach and a Sunday School party form the basis of this enchanting 1951 scene. With the fifties fashions, and the village ladies in tweeds, one almost expects Agatha Christie's Miss Marple to enter the stage.

Below The AA patrolman's sidecar parked outside Woodstock station in 1951 provides another period piece. There is no car around to need his ministrations, and he would hardly be attending to the 0-4-2T. Miss Marple would find it very interesting, and perhaps solve 'the case of the missing patrolman'. On a more serious note, the country fashions, as in the previous view, Sunday School party and AA sidecar are all points the modeller could utilise.

Rugby

Above In 1844-45, the GWR strove to reach Rugby, the gateway to the North, but the gauge wars with the LNWR intervened. Fifty years later, the creation of the London Extension of the Great Central Railway offered a new route north. At Great Western insistence, backed by a subscription of over £280,000, the GCR obtained powers in 1897 for an 8¼ mile link from the GWR at Banbury to its as yet unbuilt main line at Culworth. The GC main line opened in 1899, and the Banbury spur on 13th August 1900. Through passenger and freight developed, and GWR-engines ran north over the GCR. It may seem strange to class the GC main line as a GWR 'branch', but to omit this important feeder to the Oxford line would be quite wrong. A well groomed Hawksworth 'County', No. 1019 *County of Merioneth* heads south out of Rugby Central in 1958. Prestigious workings, such as the York-Bournemouth, survived until the demise of the GC as a through route on 5th September 1966.

Princes Risborough Branches

Below Continuing the Great Central theme, we return to the GW & GC Joint Line at Princes Risborough in time to see a '14xx' pulling out of the 'up' platform in 1951. Risboro' was the focal point of a number of local and auto services, including workings from Oxford via Thame, from Banbury, from Watlington, and from Aylesbury. As the station also handled the principal Birmingham line expresses ex-Paddington, and a range of workings from Marylebone, the quadruple track through the station area earned its keep. In this view, looking towards Paddington, we see the commodious goods yard on the left, and the connection from the south end of the station to the 'up' loop platform on the right. Today the Bicester line is singled north of Risborough, and whilst the Aylesbury line carries passengers, the Thame and Watlington lines are both truncated as freight-only spurs.

PRINCES RISBOROUGH and WATLINGTON.
(ENGINE AND BRANCH CAR, ONE CLASS ONLY.)

SINGLE LINE. Worked by Train Staff and only one engine in steam at a time, or two coupled together. Form of Staff, Round. Colour, Black.
Passenger Trains to carry "B" Headlamps. Freight Trains to carry one Headlamp in centre of buffer plank.

Week Days only.

Down Trains.

Distance M.	Distance C.	STATIONS	Ruling Gradient 1 in	Point to point times (Mins.)	Allow for Stop (Mins.)	Allow for Start (Mins.)	Freight K a.m.	Empty Auto ¶ a.m.	Freight N RR a.m.	Passenger a.m.	Freight SX p.m.	Passenger SO p.m.	Passenger p.m.	Freight SO p.m.	Passenger p.m.	Passenger p.m.	Freight p.m.
—	—	Princes Risborough .... dep.	—	—	—	1	5 30	7 57	9 20	10 22	12 20	12 40	1 55	3 55	5 48	8 0	10 15
1	52	Bledlow Bridge Halt .. „	107 F.	—	—	—	—	—	—	10 27	—	12 45	2 0	—	5 53	8 5	—
2	75	Wainhill Halt .... „	68 R.	—	—	—	—	—	—	10 30	—	12 48	2 3	—	5 56	8 8	—
3	57	Chinnor .. „	68 R.	12	1	1	CR	CR	9 30	10 33	12 34	12 51	2 6	4 9	5 59	8 11	—
5	17	Kingston Crossing Halt .. „	61 R.	—	—	—	Q	—	—	10 37	—	12 55	2 10	—	6 3	8 15	—
6	16	Aston Rowant „	116 F.	8	1	1	6 35	CR	...	10 40	—	12 58	2 13	—	6 6	8 18	CR
7	4	Lewknor Bridge Halt .... „	117 F.	—	—	—	—	—	...	10 43	—	1 1	2 16	—	6 9	8 21	—
8	75	Watlington .... arr.	78 F.	8	1	—	6 45	8 20	...	10 48	—	1 6	2 21	—	6 14	8 26	10 45

¶—May convey passengers from Princes Risborough when required.   K—Suspended.   Q Aston Rowant arrive 5.52 a.m.
N—Will run as "light engine" if required.

Up Trains.

STATIONS	Ruling Gradient 1 in	Point to point times (Mins.)	Allow for Stop (Mins.)	Allow for Start (Mins.)	Freight K a.m.	Passenger a.m.	Passenger a.m.	Engine and Van V RR a.m.	Passenger a.m.	Freight SX p.m.	Passenger SO p.m.	Passenger p.m.	Freight SO p.m.	Passenger p.m.	Freight p.m.
Watlington .... dep.	—	—	—	1	4 20	7 25	8 42		11 30		1 15	3 10		7 15	8 40
Lewknor Bridge Halt .. „	78 R.				—	7 30	8 47		11 35		1 20	3 15		7 20	Z
Aston Rowant .... „	117 R.	8	1	1	—	7 33	8 52		11 38		1 23	3 18		7 23	9 10
Kingston Crossing Halt.. „	116 F.				—	7 36	8 55	10†0	11 41		1 26	3 21		7 26	—
Chinnor .... „	61 F.	8	1	1	CR	7 40	9 0		11 45	1 18	1 30	3 25	4 55	7 30	CR
Wainhill Halt .. „	68 F.				—	7 43	9 3		11 48		1 33	3 28		7 33	—
Bledlow Bridge Halt .... „	68 F.				—	7 46	9 6	10†15	11 51		1 36	3 31		7 36	—
Princes Risborough .. arr.	107 R.	10	1	—	4 48	7 51	9 11		11 56	1 30	1 41	3 36	5 5	7 41	9 30

K—Suspended.   V—Will run as "light engine" if required.   Z—Aston Rowant arrive 8.50 p.m.

Watlington

Above The Western Region 'Service' Time Tables, from 31st May to 26th September 1948, recall not just the freight and passenger services, but details of the train staff, lamp codes, mileages, running times and ruling gradients, for the Watlington branch.

Below Watlington station, looking towards Princes Risborough in 1951. The coal stage, opposite the auto coach, is worthy of study, as is the corrugated iron carriage shed on the right. The loco shed used to be on the spur which diverges off the run round by the coal stage, but was burned down in 1906 and never replaced.

Little Kimble

Above The Princes Risborough-Aylesbury line was originally part of the GWR, but became joint property in 1907. The principal intermediate station was Little Kimble. The station buildings, although converted to a house, have survived.

Below left An even more interesting survival is the GWR station nameboard, which despite years of neglect, is still instantly readable.

Aylesbury

Below right At Aylesbury the station was under GW & GC, and Metropolitan & GC control, a 'handle' which just about doubled the size of the Private Road Notice!

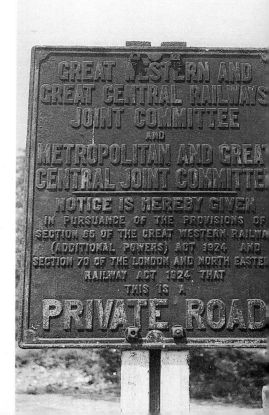

Above A GWR 'Metro' tank with large water tanks and volute springs, drifts southwards through Aylesbury station in 1929.

Below Aylesbury, looking south towards Marylebone and Paddington, with the GWR Princes Risborough platform to the right, by the loco shed, on 3rd June 1966.

Leamington to Shrewsbury

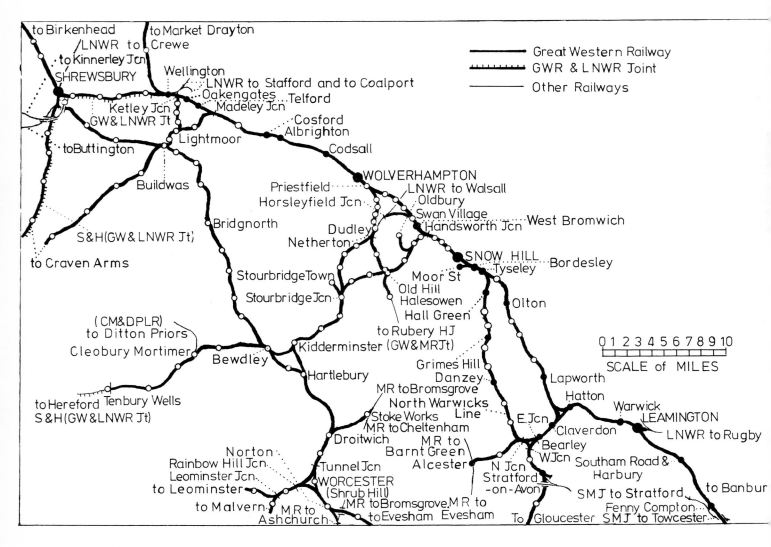

The old Birmingham line, from Didcot to Leamington was predominantly double track, with a string of pretty little country stations, now mostly gone, whilst the Joint Line and the Bicester cut-off were also double track, though in this case, there was considerable suburban development, at least as far as Princes Risborough.

West of Leamington, the line assumed a different character, with long stretches of quadruple track, to cope with the Birmingham suburban traffic. A subsidiary route, the 'North Warwicks' ran parallel to the main line but two or three miles to the west, with the lines merging at Tyseley. The outlying stations served the Birmingham 'stockbroker' belt, whilst the houses crowded closer together as one neared central Birmingham. Quadruple track extended a short distance north of Snow Hill, the line running through industrial districts to Wolverhampton and Oxley, whence it turned west to Wellington and Shrewsbury passing through attractive countryside once more. The section from Leamington to Shrewsbury, approximately one third of the total mileage from Paddington to Birkenhead, generated a substantial slice of total traffic, both freight and passenger.

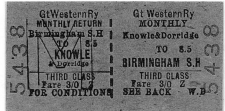

Leamington Spa

Above The '36xx' 2-4-2Ts appeared during the Dean-Churchward transition, and were the first significant attempt by the Great Western to produce something larger than the 0-4-2T or 2-4-0T for suburban work. Thirty were built from 1900 to 1903, after which Churchward concentrated on his small and large Prairie tanks. Their principal stronghold was the Birmingham area, and in 1922 six were based at Leamington for the south-side suburban turns. A further sixteen were based at other sheds with Birmingham runs. No. 3616 is seen at the east end of Leamington station, no doubt shunting empty stock, prior to a morning Birmingham turn about 1928. The '36xx' tanks succumbed to the fleet of new Prairies built by Collett, all going between 1930 and 1934.

Below One of the Collett Prairies, No. 5544, a 4575 series engine sent new to Stourbridge in 1928, bustles along importantly at the head of the Stratford slip from the 'down' 3.40pm about 1933. The small Prairies of 4500 and 4575 classes were never plentiful in the Birmingham area, although Stourbridge, Tyseley and Stafford Road acquired a few, in 1927-28. Later they tended to drift away to other areas, being replaced by the more powerful 5101 class tanks. This portrait of Leamington station gives a further opportunity to study the truncated remains of the old train shed, and to wonder that the Great Western accepted such an unimpressive structure at a significant station for so long.

Above The vantage point is not very different from the previous plate, but other than for the quadruple tracks through the station, the two scenes have little in common. No. 4943 *Marrington Hall,* a Reading engine, heads in the Warwick direction with a class C fitted freight in 1951. The fireman has taken advantage of the long descent from Harbury to build up a good head of steam and No. 4943 is blowing off gently. She will need that careful preparation very shortly, for although the line falls for a mile or so, it then starts almost six miles of ascent, much of it at a merciless 1 in 103/105. The boardwalk in the foreground was for the use of the wheeltappers, whose activities are an abiding memory which the authors have of Leamington Spa station.

Below The north end sidings and passenger bay on the 'down' side of the station provided a convenient place to dump all sorts of stock. Here we see a Birmingham local set in BR suburban red in the 'down' bay, and an auto trailer, No. W66 in carmine and cream. This was built as a diagram L 74 ft branch auto trailer and was fitted with extra large buffer heads, because of its extreme length. One of Leamington's ubiquitous 5101 tanks, No. 4112, is on the nearest road. This Prairie tank spent most of her life in the Leamington area, being sent new to the shed in 1936, and was still there fifteen years later. It ended its days at Banbury in 1962.

Above In 1956, the Russian Bolshoi Ballet visited the United Kingdom, the first cultural exchange with the Soviet Union. As a part of their programme, the party visited Stratford-upon-Avon, home of the Royal Shakespeare Company. A special train, double headed by Nos 5060 *Earl of Berkeley* and 5065 *Newport Castle* ran from Paddington on 21st October 1956. The train paused for water at Leamington Spa. Needless to say, both engines were immaculately turned out, though one wonders how the selection of an 'Earl' would have gone down with the party commissars!

Below The drastic increase in freight on the GWR during World War II led to the appearance of Riddles', Ministry of Supply 2-8-0s, Stanier LMS-designed 2-8-0s, and the U.S. Army Transportation Corp engines. A batch of Riddles engines were loaned to the GWR in 1944-45, and a further group from 1946-47. One of the latter, No. 77408, heads an afternoon freight up the grade past Leamington cattle dock in 1947. She is still carrying the Westinghouse pump fitted to these engines for overseas duties, and removed from those which came into BR ownership later on.

A 'Castle' or 'King' at the head of an express, or a '28xx' on a freight epitomises the GWR to most enthusiasts, and the lowly pannier is the veriest trifle. The reality was very different. Without the *thousand-plus* 0-6-0 tanks in stock for the last fifty years of the company's life, it could hardly have functioned! The mileage figures show why. Out of 98.5 million engine miles in 1938, 20.3 million miles, or more than one in five – were freight shunting! We have purposely chosen this classic portrait of a GWR yard scene for this feature. No. 2772, a Swindon 4ft 7½in open cab pannier of the 2721 class, shunts the 'down' yard at Leamington in 1947. Built in September 1900, she was the sole *old time* pannier at Leamington, and with her open cab, kept on yard duties.

An amusing reflection upon this duty is that, in the fifties, an engine worked off shed each night to sit in the yard, though it had no work to perform. One local officer finally queried this and, after patient digging, discovered that the engine was sent off shed in case of an air raid by the Luftwaffe. The air raid precaution lasted about three times as long as the war had!

Warwick

Above As the shadows lengthen, and Warwick station slumbers in the afternoon sun, we look towards Leamington shortly after the War. A horse box in the 'down' bay records how important such traffic once was.

Below An early '45xx' tank, No. 4546, enters Warwick in 1937, with a varied Stratford local, comprising an LNER horse box, a magnificent Dean clerestory bogie, and a modern Collett coach. What a marvellous mixture!

Opposite top No. 4933 *Himley Hall* storms through Warwick on a class F unfitted freight in 1937, her crew relieved that she has a clear road, as the worst part of Hatton bank, a brief stretch at 1 in 100 lies just west of the station. The 3,500 gallon tender carries a 'shirt button' motif.

Opposite below The 'Western' class 2,700 hp C-C diesel hydraulics, introduced in 1961, were the last flowering of Great Western independence. No. D1022 *Western Sentinel* roars through Warwick in 1963, At their birth, the 'Westerns' were hated by GW devotees, being seen as a threat to Swindon steam. By the time of their own demise, they too had myriads of devotees.

Opposite top 'ROD' 2-8-0, No. 3048, whistles vigorously, as she drifts down the grade into Warwick station at the head of an empty Stewarts & Lloyds iron ore train shortly before the War. The mix of steel hoppers and timber-bodied wagons is of interest, as are the differing S&L private owner liveries. In the foreground, a pair of Foster & Co. private owners await unloading into the narrow gauge trucks serving the short private siding. One wonders how many passengers on the adjoining main line ever noticed this tiny narrow gauge feeder. Again, it is a feature which modellers could well emulate, with a diorama of men transhipping minerals, and the n.g. trucks being moved by manpower or perhaps a horse!

Opposite below As a solitary workman shovels coal out of the wagons in the foreground, a gleaming 'Saint', No. 2914 *Saint Augustine*, has started the long climb from Warwick to Hatton. She has steam to spare and will not be troubled by the relatively modest load. Warwick station is visible in the distance, and an engine sits ready in the 'down' bay to bank any trains needing assistance.

Below As if to prove that age has not dimmed her resolve, No. 1748, a 655 class large 'Wolverhampton Pannier', still with an open backed cab, throws out a hearty column of smoke, as she slogs up the 1 in 105 bank through Hatton cutting in the summer of 1939. Staunch though her efforts are, they pale into insignificance when compared to the pall of smoke vomited forth by the banker, a large, and very exuberant 5100 class Prairie.

With a relief line available, it is surprising that No. 1748, with its lowly class K freight, should have been permitted on to the main line, so it may be that the banker is anxious to get the train clear of the main line ere a 'King' or 'Castle' is due. It was in locations such as this, where faced with a real challenge, that the steam locomotive was at its most spectacular. Wonderful though the preserved lines are, it is sad that future generations of enthusiasts can only savour moments such as these through photographs.

Hatton

Above Hatton Junction, looking towards Birmingham in 1956. Points of interest include the nameboard on the 'down' platform with its comprehensive 'junction' details – those for the closed Bearley-Alcester line being deleted, the old coach body on the 'up' platform, and the diamond pattern blue paving bricks.

Below The crew of 0-6-2T No. 5634 are taking it easy as she beats the bank and is signalled on to the Birmingham line with a trip freight. In the background is yet another horse box. The line in the foreground is the Stratford platform.

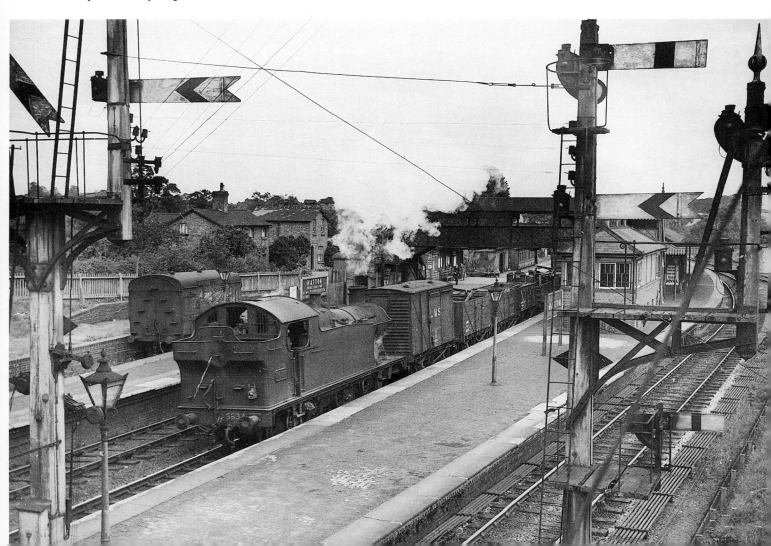

Above Between 1943 and 1945 Swindon built 80 Stanier 8F 2-8-0s for the LMS, all of them being initially loaned back to the GWR. No. 8462, an Ebbw Junction engine, was built in December 1944, and stayed on the GWR until May 1947. She is starting a class H empty ore train away from the 'up' loop at Hatton Junction in 1946.

Below A Pontypool Road 'Toad' has come to grief, blocking the 'up' and 'down' Stratford lines at Hatton Junction in 1946. As a railcar waits in the 'up' loop and a 'Hall' passes by on the main, the breakdown gang decide how to tackle the job, the head gear, soft hat, bowler or cloth cap being an infallible guide to rank!

Above A 3-car dmu in railcar green with the original 'feathers' swings on to the Birmingham line at Hatton Junction about 1960. Hatton South signal box is visible through the right hand arch of the road bridge. The lines to the left are the Birmingham main lines; those to the right the double track branch to Stratford. To the right of the bridge is one of the diamond-shaped bridge restriction plates which contained an interminable essay in very small lettering about what could or could not use the bridge. Any driver conscientious enough to stop at each bridge to read such plates would make slow progress indeed!

Below The superelevation is obvious, as a 'King' pounds through Hatton North Junction with a 'down' express about 1960. The 'up' refuge loop commences beyond the footbridge, whilst the curve from Hatton West Junction comes in to the right of the train. With Hatton bank surmounted, the crew have a respite before the much easier climb from Rowington to Solihull, and the few hundred yards of 1 in 45 part way between Bordesley and Snow Hill.

Lapworth

Lapworth was the next station after Hatton, and marked the commencement of the quadruple track section as far as the divergence of the Snow Hill and Moor St lines in Birmingham. Plans to widen from Rowington Junction, between Hatton and Lapworth, to Olton were drafted before WWI, but put on ice, and not resurrected until 1929 as a government-supported unemployment relief scheme. The work, initially budgeted at £400,000, was completed in 1933, though the lines stopped at Lapworth. Although only eight miles in length, it augmented the quadruple trackage from Didcot to Chester by a third. We are looking from the 'up' main towards Birmingham in June 1971. The relief lines, which were removed upon the eclipse of the GW as a main route, lay to the left, and were unusual in that whilst there was a connection from the 'down' main to the 'down' relief south of the station, the 'up' relief was a dead end, for turn-back workings. Further retrenchment saw the buildings shorn of canopies, surely a retrograde move anywhere, but especially in the 'stockbroker' belt where the traveller will expect high standards!

The station forecourt at Lapworth in June 1971. Stations such as this, which had to be enlarged to handle suburban traffic, or for quadrupling, were in marked contrast to the older 'country' stations such as Aynho or Harbury.

Olton

The first Olton station dated from 1869, but was replaced before the First World War, when the southern approaches to Birmingham were remodelled, and the main line quadrupled as far as Olton. Further extensions hung fire until the thirties, as noted. An early *Intermediate Block,* or 'IB' signalling system, using power worked semaphore signals, with motors on the posts, saved the need for a manned signal box. Colour lights were much more common in such situations. We see the station on 13th January 1966.

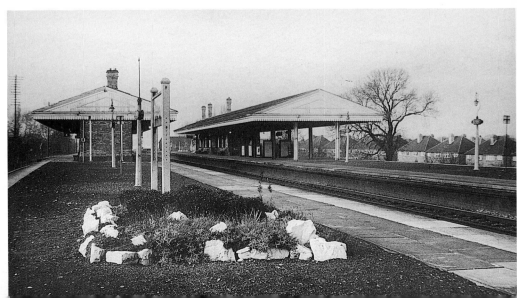

Tyseley

Above The afternoon 'up' 'Blue Pullman' accelerates south through Tyseley on New Year's Day, 1965. One realised that the reign of Great Western steam was drawing to a close, but it was inconceivable at the time that the 'Blue Pullmans' would follow steam into oblivion within a very few years. The main and relief lines curve away to the left of Tyseley South box, and the 'up' and 'down' North Warwick lines swing away sharply to the right beyond the box. A maze of connections link main, relief and North Warwicks lines.

Below A Riddles Standard 9F class 2-10-0, No. 92150, is wreathed in steam, as she heads a heavy coal train, of 16T steel mineral wagons, southwards through Tyseley on 1st January 1965. A couple of youthful train spotters make notes from the platform, for all too soon this will be history. The chimneys and tall industrial premises dominate the Birmingham skyline in a view which emphasises the nature of the GWR main line in this area.

Above To generations of locomen, the allocation of a steed for the day, whether via 'book' or 'board', made all the difference between a good or bad day, for no two engines were the same, and a locomotive ex-works was a different matter from one due for shopping. The LMR-style *Train Arrangements Board* at Tyseley shed for Friday 30th October 1964 recalls the days when the shed master at any large depot put scores of steam engines into traffic daily. It is also a roll call of engines familiar on the Birmingham line in the last days of steam, and includes five 'Castles', Nos 7013, 7014, 7019, 7023 and 7029, together with many other stalwarts, such as Nos 3635, 6633, 6833, 6879, 6926, 7805 and 7915.

Below Earlier in this book, we have seen gleaming 'Saints', 'Castles' and 'Kings', but by 1964-65, it was all very different. No. 7014 *Caerhays Castle* is parked on one of the 'extension' spurs at the back of Tyseley shed on 1st January 1965, by which time any GWR engine with number plates, let alone nameplates, was a rarity! All 'Castles' with 3 and 4-row superheaters gained mechanical lubricators, but five engines, including No. 7014, received Davies & Metcalfe Patent Valveless lubricators, the lubricator being on the running plate ahead of the steam pipe, with its reservoir mounted on the smokebox above the steampipe. *Caerhays Castle* was withdrawn in February 1965.

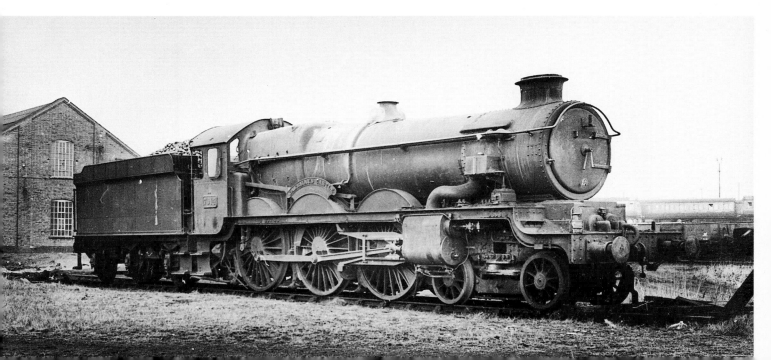

Above A large steam shed had an ethereal quality, hard to define and impossible to recapture under 'preservation'. Smoke and steam eddied around, however good the ventilation. There were the smells; of hot oil, grease, steam, smoke and coal. There were the sounds; men talking, engines moving, hot metal contracting as engines cooled down, of a fitter gently caressing some engine with a hammer. There were also the engines. The first GWR-built 0-6-0Ts were side tanks, but by 1864, the company had opted for the saddle tank, hundreds of which were to appear. No. 2005, seen at Tyseley on 13th October 1935, is an 850/1901 class 'Wolverhampton' small tank dating from 1892. She was converted to panniers in 1937 and withdrawn in December 1944.

Tyseley Shed

Below No. 2104 slumbers in Tyseley shed on 13th October 1935, as sunlight filters through the steam and smoke. This 0-6-0PT was built as a 2101 class saddle tank with domeless Belpaire boiler in 1902, and was one of several engines to retain the domeless boiler when converted to panniers in 1927, running thus until 1937. She reached the 'A' power group (18,500 lb) with 15 lb to spare!

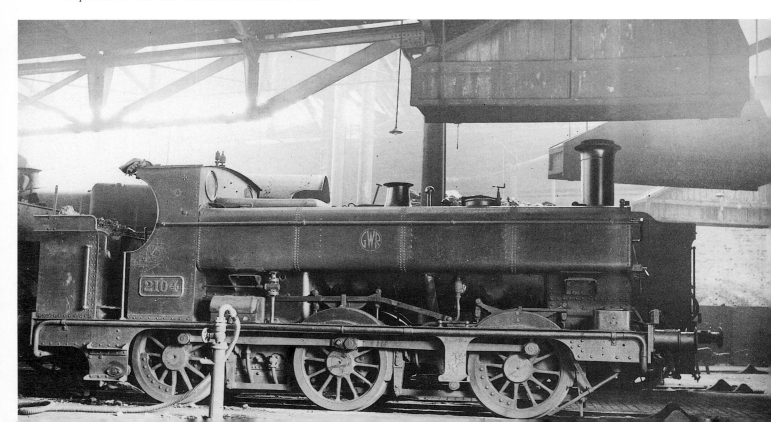

Bordesley

Bordesley station was located just short of the Coventry Road bridge, west of which the line was carried on continuous viaduct to the vicinity of Moor St. Bordesley station is depicted on 1st June 1971.

Bordesley North box adjoined the 'up' main line, and was located where the abortive viaduct connection to the LNWR at Curzon St. commenced. As the line was never laid in to the LNWR, the GWR eventually used it as a cattle dock, reached from the tracks disappearing behind the 49-lever timber box in this portrait, taken from the 'down' main on 20th March 1966.

Snow Hill

The northern approach to Snow Hill, looking from the 'up' platform, No. 8, towards Wolverhampton on 30th October 1964. As well as the two through lines and platform roads apparent here, there were a pair of bays at the north ends of both platforms, although the 'up' bays were seldom used, and there were additional platform lines on the outer face of each island. North of the station the main lines were to the right, and the relief roads to the left, quadruple track extending out to Handsworth.

Above As the p.w. staff busy themselves by Snow Hill North box, an amazing structure mounted upon a pedestal, left, No. 6001 *King Edward VII* arrives from the North with an 'up' special in 1959-60. The train is routed from the 'up' main to the main face of the 'up' island, platform No. 8. The 3-way point in the foreground leads, left to right, to the 'down' relief, 'down' north headshunt and 'down' main. The 'Toad' brake van, No. 56291, never turned a wheel for years!

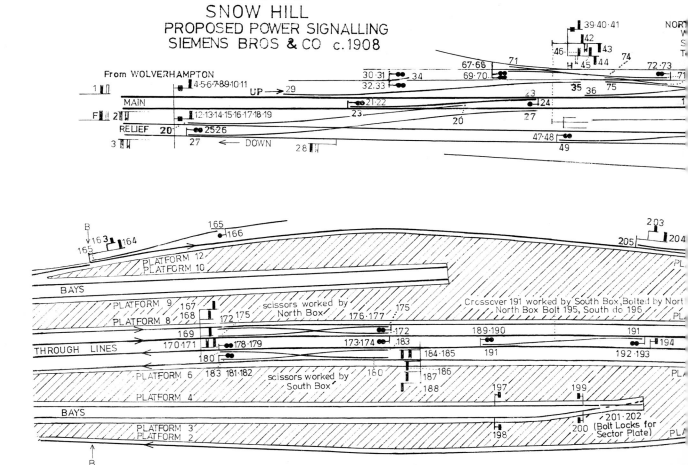

BIRMINGHAM
SNOW HILL
PROPOSED POWER SIGNALLING
SIEMENS BROS & CO c.1908

No. 5606, a 5600 class 0-6-2T, awaits the road with an 'up' trip on 30th October 1964, carrying Tyseley shed's final 2A code adopted in September 1963. Scissors crossovers provided connections between the through and platform lines in the middle of the station, but from the 1930s were seldom used, due to increasing train lengths. Note the central ventilation gap in the overall roof.

Below From the turn of the century the GWR drastically upgraded its Birmingham network, Snow Hill being completely remodelled, and an early power signalling system adopted. Our signal plan is a Siemens Bros engineer's proposal plan of about 1908, with signals and points numbered sequentially for both boxes. The North box was installed in 1909, and the South box in 1913. As with other early power frames, there were problems, and major rebuilding was necessary at the North box by 1915, although the installation struggled on until 1960 when a modern panel replaced it. The Snow Hill-Moor St. line closed in March 1968, and the Wolverhampton service ended on 6th March 1972, the station site lingering as a car park until 1976/77. At that time, the idea of a 'new' Snow Hill seemed unlikely, but that is another story.

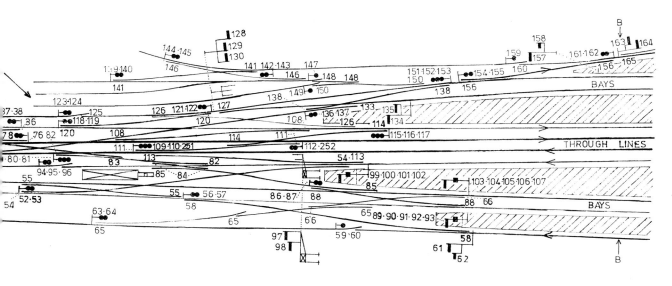

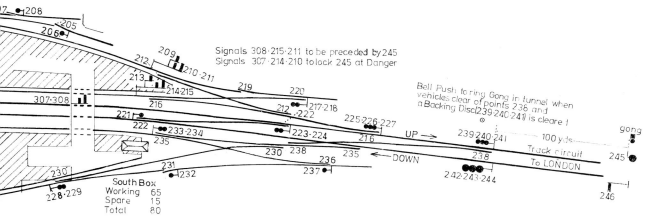

Signals 308·215·211 to be preceded by 245
Signals 307·214·210 to lock 245 at Danger

Bell Push to ring Gong in tunnel when vehicles clear of points 236 and a Backing Disc(239·240·241) is cleared

South Box
Working 65
Spare 15
Total 80

West Bromwich

From Birmingham to Wolverhampton, the main line threaded its way through the heartland of the industrial West Midlands, with a succession of works and factories. West Bromwich, best known for its soccer team, lay roughly midway along the section, and is depicted upon closure in March 1972.

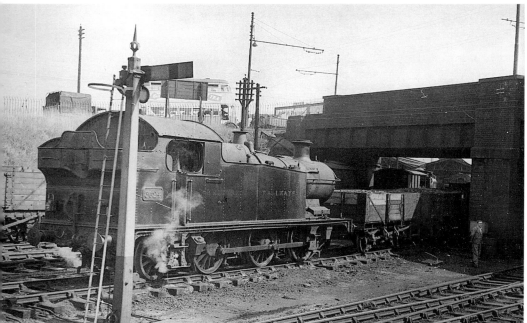

Wolverhampton

No. 5624, 0-6-2T shunts near Wolverhampton (Low Level) station in 1952, bearing GWR-style 'BRITISH RAILWAYS' serif lettering on her tanks. The bunker recess, and original tall safety valve casing can be seen to advantage.

There are few passengers, but plenty of parcels at Wolverhampton (Low Level) station on 31st October 1964. Through services between Paddington and Birkenhead succumbed in 1967. In 1968 Shrewsbury services were switched to the High Level station, as had been the original 1850's idea, and the Snow Hill service went next, but Low Level soldiered on as a parcels depot, and in the 1980s became the subject of an abortive preservation project – a chequered career indeed!

Dunstall Park

Above The Shrewsbury & Birmingham diverged from the OW&WR ½ mile west of Low Level, and after passing below the LNWR 'Stour Valley' viaduct, served Dunstall Park station, which was opened on 1st December 1896. The environs of the station, depicted on 31st October 1964 included Stafford Road shed and works, Oxley shed, a gas works and a long viaduct; *Park* was something of a misnomer!

Stafford Road Shed

Below No. 3223, a Dean 'Barnum' class 2-4-0, with extended frames to fit piston valves, is outside the old Stafford Road shed on 11th October 1933. It is fascinating to recall that these engines rubbed shoulders with the broad gauge motive power and 'Kings', 'Castles' and 'Halls'. The old shed is another marvellous antiquity.

Above Swindon and GWR steam are often seen as synonymous, but until the end of the broad gauge in 1892, Stafford Road was the true 'home' of GWR 'narrow gauge' power for both Joseph Armstrong and William Dean had carried the gospel of 4ft 8½in from Stafford Road. It is appropriate that our first view of the 1932 erecting shop at Stafford Road should depict a Dean engine, 'Bulldog' No. 3309 *Maristow,* probably on her last shopping before withdrawal in 1934.

Below A 'Star', No. 4021 *British Monarch*, also receives attention at Stafford Road. The original Shrewsbury & Birmingham Railway works opened in 1849, with a further site being added by the GWR, and a brand new erecting shop on a third site appearing in 1932. It was a commodious building, but transfer of much GW mileage to the London Midland Region led to closure in June 1964.

Oxley Shed

Right Stafford Road shed had succumbed even earlier than the works – in September 1963, with surviving engines being concentrated at the nearby Oxley shed. No. 6815. *Frilford Grange* is caught on the shed approach tracks on 31st October 1964. By this time, theft of plates was becoming common, and an engine with a full set was a rarity. A locomotive which was also clean was even rarer – and *very* welcome. No. 6815 survived until November 1965.

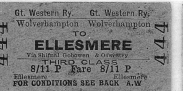

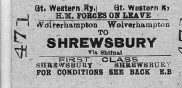

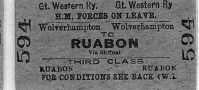

Wolverhampton Tickets

Above A selection of GWR tickets from Wolverhampton recall how strategically placed the town was for journeys to the North, South, East and West.

Right A large Prairie, No. 4148, pauses on the shed approach at Oxley on 31st October 1964.

Codsall

Once clear of Wolverhampton, the line ran in a westerly direction to Shrewsbury, with the section from Wellington onwards being joint with the LMS. The 19½ miles from Wolverhampton to Wellington were 'pure' Great Western, being all that the Shrewsbury & Birmingham Railway built by itself. The Shrewsbury-Wellington-Oakengates section opened on 1st June 1849, and the Oakengates-Wolverhampton portion on 12th November. Although a GWR main line, carrying loads far heavier than anything envisaged at its birth, some traces of the original work still survive, as at Codsall, where the beams carrying the ornate parapet walling proclaim their ancestry – 'Thomas Perry & Son, Highfields Foundry 1848'.

In the early days, passenger access was invariably by means of timber crossings, which survived as barrow-ways long after most stations were provided with footbridges. The 1880s were a prolific period for footbridge construction, as evidenced by the date cast upon the support bracket for the footbridge at Codsall. The GWR monogram is typical of the Victorian era.

The unusual platform levels at Codsall reveal the age of these mildly Italianate buildings. Most of the platform is of normal height, but part way along the buildings it dips down, and even this was not the intended height, for there is a further depression by the door from the booking hall on to the platform. When platforms were raised, low floor levels within the existing buildings were a perennial problem, sometimes solved by a slope down to the doors, but more commonly, by means of steps and railings.

Albrighton

Albrighton was the next station on the S&BR, and was architecturally similar to Codsall, with an Italianate main building with round headed door openings and windows, the latter grouped in twins or triplets. The sylvan surroundings to the station reveal that even today, the quiet Shropshire countryside is little affected by modern life.

As at Codsall, the platform is carried over a road-bridge, the parapet of which is visible to the left of the footbridge stairway. The footbridge is of classic GWR style, and would proclaim the ownership of the station irrespective of the GWR monograms. Before the abandonment of wayside goods yards, stations such as this possessed modest freight facilities, and quite often a refuge siding to enable freight trains to get out of the way of the passenger workings. At Albrighton, there was a refuge siding on the 'up' side, holding 40 wagons. With increasing train lengths, this was somewhat restrictive, but as the box was open only 'as required' it was more important to lengthen refuge sidings or loops which were available continuously.

For the modeller, it is frequently the details which are hard to resolve. This view is included principally for the platform surfaces. On the right we have patterned deep blue-black paving bricks as a platform surfacing, with the larger edging bricks finishing the job. In the distance the bricks give way to paving slabs. On the far platform the ramp is in paving bricks, but both edges are provided with paving slabs. The platform itself is asphalt or tarmac, with edging stone slabs. Finally, the paving bricks themselves differ, some being patterned, others plain. The only common platform surfacings not displayed are timber or loose gravel.

Cosford

RAF Cosford is perhaps best known today for the large aerospace museum which has been developed, and which includes such famous aircraft as the Spitfire, Mosquito, Meteor, Canberra and Dakota. It is still, however, a working RAF depot as well and, with the S&BR passing within yards of the base, it was inevitable that a halt would be provided to handle the service personnel. The line runs on an embankment and the platforms and buildings are carried on brick and timber pillars, as is apparent in this portrait of the 'down' buildings of Cosford station which, incidentally, was taken just a few feet from one of the camp gates.

The main booking office is a brick structure at road level on the 'up' side. The station opened as Cosford Aerodrome Halt in the late thirties, but was upgraded, and renamed Cosford on 28th November 1940. The Great Western annual report for 1938 reveals that some preliminary work was done in 1938, with more in 1939-40.

Timber waiting rooms were provided on both platforms, which were also timber built, for economy and lightness, given the embankment site. We are looking towards Wolverhampton on 25th August 1988. The ground-level booking office can just be seen to the left of the 'up' buildings, whilst RAF Cosford lies to the right of the line. Cosford handled public goods traffic until 7th September 1964.

Immediately to the west of the platforms, 'up' and 'down' goods loops were laid in, each capable of holding a 60-wagon train. The hangars of RAF Cosford flank the line from the 'down' platform to beyond the signal cabin in the middle distance, with further RAF buildings on the other side of the line.

Telford

The area around Oakengates, Shifnal and Wellington was designated Telford New Town with a population target of over 200,000 by the early 1980s. At first, it was projected as the 'Motorway Town', but second thoughts prevailed, and BR agreed to provide a new station, entitled Telford Central, on the site of the old Hollinswood sidings, between Oakengates and Shifnal. A target date of 1975 was over-optimistic, the station not opening until 12th May 1986. A theme which dominates this book is the inexorable run down, under BR, of the Great Western route to Birmingham and the Mersey, so it is pleasant to record the appearance of a new station, even if not of GWR quality.

Oakengates

Oakengates station, could scarcely be a greater contrast, for we return to the formative years of railway architecture, with a main building virtually at ground level. Indeed, so low was the floor level, that when the platforms were raised it was necessary to provide the usual sunken entrance. In modern times, an enclosed passageway led from the building to the platform avoiding the risk of passengers overlooking an unprotected step, and falling.

Wellington

Opposite top From Wellington to Shrewsbury, the S&BR was forced by Parliament to join forces with the rival Shropshire Union Railways & Canal Co., and build a joint line. As the S&BR fell into the GWR camp, whilst the SUR was an LNWR affiliate, the result could have pleased neither Paddington nor Euston! The joint section opened on 1st June 1849. Over the next twenty years, further routes radiated north and south. We look from the 'down' platform at Wellington in 1951 as No. 7017 *G. J. Churchward* pauses with a Birmingham express. A Prairie tank has just added a milk tank to the rear of the train. Two more Prairies and a pannier tank are in the vicinity of the 3-road GWR loco shed on the right of the view.

Right Although use of the *shirt button* logo ceased for rolling stock after 1942, it continued to surface elsewhere, as with this 1946 handbill, promoting day excursions to Wellington. Older readers will be familiar with pounds, shillings and pence, but for the younger enthusiast, the 4 shilling fare from Bilston is 20 pence, for a 40 mile round trip. The third class return between Paddington and Birkenhead was 39s 10d, or £1.99 at this time!

Opposite below The graceful columns, with their elegant cast spandrels create a cloistered effect in his portrait of the 'down' platform at Wellington in 1976. Sadly modern designers seem to have lost the ability to produce such harmonious and pleasing structures. The clock in the foreground is truly eye-catching, but what a shame it does not tell the same time as the further clock (which is correct)!

CHEAP TICKETS

THURSDAYS

AUGUST 1st to SEPTEMBER 26th
(inclusive)

DAY EXCURSION BOOKINGS

TO

WELLINGTON

(FOR THE WREKIN)

FROM					Depart	Return Fares Third Class		RETURN SAME DAY	
					a.m.	s.	d.	p.m.	p.m.
Birmingham (Snow Hill)	..	..	..	..	8 22	5	8	7 5	8A 56
Handsworth and Smethwick	..	..	..	..	8 28	5	3	7A 5	8 56
West Bromwich	..	..	..	..	8 33	4	11	7A 5	8 56
Dudley	..	..	..	..	8 A19	4	7	7A 5	8 56
Wednesbury	..	..	..	..	8 40	4	5	7A 5	8 56
Bilston (G.W.)	..	..	..	..	8. 45	4	0	7A 5	8 56
Priestfield	..	..	..	..	9 7	3	11	7A 5	8 56
Wolverhampton (Low Level)	..	..	..	..	9 0	3	7	7 5	8 56
Dunstall Park	..	..	..	..	9 23	3	4	7 5	8 56

A—Change at Wolverhampton (L.L.)

Children under Three years of age, Free ; Three and under Fourteen years, Half-fare

NOTICE AS TO CONDITIONS.—TICKETS ARE AVAILABLE FOR DAY OF ISSUE ONLY AND ARE NOT TRANSFERABLE—BREAK OF JOURNEY NOT ALLOWED.

These tickets are issued subject to the conditions of issue of Ordinary Passenger Tickets where applicable and also to the special conditions as set out in the Ticket, etc., Regulations, By-Laws and General Notices. Luggage allowances are as set out in these general notices.

TICKETS ISSUED AND DATED IN ADVANCE AT STATIONS AND OFFICES.

Any further information may be obtained from

Mr. A. V. R. BROWN, Divisional Superintendent, Snow Hill Station, Birmingham. *Telephone Central* 5071 (*extension* "Enquiries") or from

Mr. GILBERT MATTHEWS, Superintendent of the Line, Paddington Station, W.2. *Telephone*: Paddington 7000 (*extension* "Enquiries" 8.0 a.m. to 10.0 p.m.).

Paddington Station, July, 1946.   JAMES MILNE, General Manager.

B.H. 31/23; B.H; 7,000;   Printed in Great Britain by Joseph Wones Ltd.,.West Bromwich ; also Birmingham and London.

Although the LMS and GWR shared passenger facilities at Wellington, each had its own goods depot. They were west of the station, the GWR yard being on the 'down' side. Access was via Wellington No. 4 signal box, but before the signalman could admit a train to the yard, he had to clear it with the GWR inspector or shunter. His method of contacting that worthy was quaint, for he blew 3 + 3 blasts on a shunting horn out of the window. This scenario, a cross between Robin Hood and Colonel Stephens, was not a local expedient but official LNWR & GWR Joint procedure!

GREAT WESTERN RAILWAY.

(111)

Parcels Way-bill, No.＿＿＿＿ WELLINGTON (Salop) to ＿＿＿＿

＿＿＿＿ o'clock Train, ＿＿＿＿ 187＿

WATERLOW & SONS LIMITED, Printers, London Wall, London.

No. of Parcel.	Description.	NAME.	ADDRESS.	Paid Through. £ s. d.	Paid on. £ s. d.	Paid. £ s. d.	To Pay. £ s. d.	Remarks.
1								
2								
3								
4								
5								
6								
			TOTAL...					

The existence of a second Wellington, just west of Taunton on the Bristol & Exeter line, was a potential source of error, and the northern town was duly labelled Wellington (Salop) on waybills, invoices etc. The 'hardware' of the railway business – locomotives, carriages etc – is so fascinating that we sometimes overlook the vast amount of paperwork which was needed to keep the whole machine running. The dispatch of a single item from one station to another involved documentation for the sender, entry in the station goods and cash books (if paid by sender), the production of a waybill and an invoice. The sending station then had to account for the item with all other traffic that day to its district office. The receiving station had to provide documentation for the consignee; it might have to collect charges. It too had to enter up freight received and cash books. In 1937 the average receipts *per ton* for merchandise was 11s 3d (56p). As many consignments were well under the ton, the railways must have lost heavily upon much of their freight business even then, but recouped it from the volume traffics. This Victorian waybill from Wellington must represent the tip of an iceberg of unbelievable size, for without such humble pieces of paper the goods system could never have functioned at all.

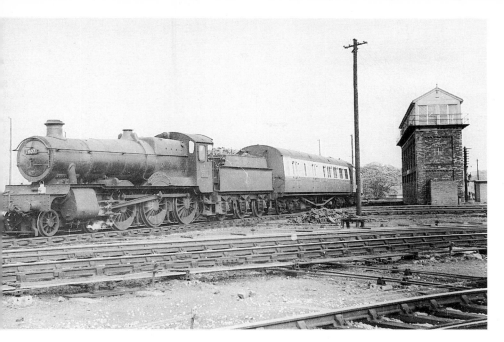

Shrewsbury

A narrow corridor of land between a Norman castle and a prison, crossed by a road and a wide river, is not the ideal location for a major station. If you throw in junctions which must begin before the end of the platform ramps at *both* ends of the station, add a lot of through traffic, summer Saturday holiday trains and then say it has to be run by two companies you have a situation calculated to drive any railwayman to despair. You also have Shrewsbury station.

Top No. 7807 *Compton Manor* drifts into Shrewsbury station at the head of an express from Wolverhampton in the early fifties, passing the tall LNWR-designed Severn Bridge Junction box, which controlled the vital junction south of the platforms. This juxtaposition of GWR and LNWR was characteristic of Shrewsbury, giving added interest to this cramped and fascinating station. The near tracks are for Welshpool, Hereford and Worcester (via the Severn Valley). An avoiding curve from the Wolverhampton line to this group passes behind the signal cabin, to produce a triangular junction. The track disappearing round the far end of the box is to a turntable in the triangle!

Centre No. 3273 *Mounts Bay* a 3252 'Duke' class 5ft 7½in Dean 4-4-0, blows off vigorously under the train shed at Shrewsbury in 1931. The 'Dukes' were built for Cornwall, but gravitated to the Cambrian main line after the Grouping.

Left Our first view caught *Compton Manor* entering Shrewsbury; this time, No. 5099 *Compton Castle*, pilots a 'Grange' from Hereford. The scissors crossover at the right is at the outer end of the west bays.

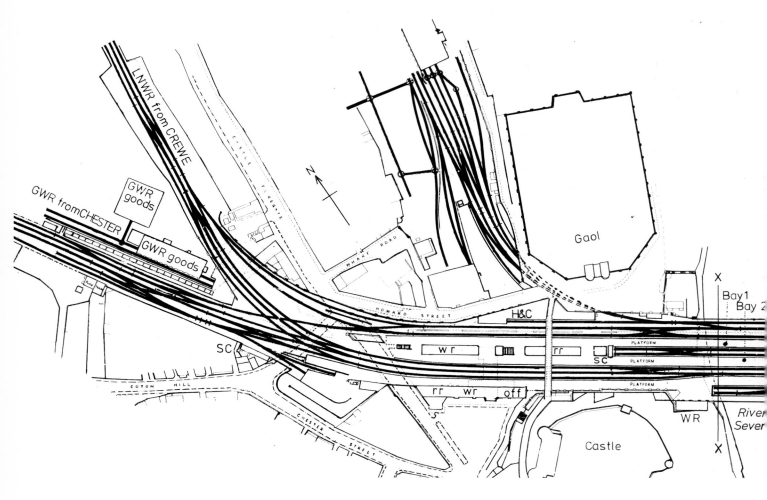

No. 7036 *Taunton Castle* pulls away from Shrewsbury with a Hereford express in the early fifties, prior to the removal of the train shed and south-end footbridge. The scissors crossover by the end of the bays is visible. Officialdom got into a terrible muddle with platform numbers at Shrewsbury, sometimes referring to platform and bays 1 to 4 (as per our plan). More helpfully, the platforms were numbered sequentially from the south, 'bay 4' being platform 1; bay 3 – platform 2, and the principal through platforms, Nos 3/4. No. 7036 is leaving from platform 4. The remaining two bays (platform 5/6) and through line 7 are obscured.

Of all the major stations between Paddington and Birkenhead, Shrewsbury is one of the most complex, on account of its numerous junctions. The photographs in this section cover the south end of the station. The north end will be dealt with in the Shrewsbury – Birkenhead section. At the north end of the station, the GWR goods depot nestles in the V of the Chester and Crewe lines, whilst the LNWR depot adjoins the gaol! Crewe Junction box, which controls the connections at this end of the station, appears a very low box to the passenger, but is in actuality a very tall cabin, as the line is carried far above street level. The turntable at the south end was so close to the avoiding curve that before turning an engine, the signalman at Severn Bridge Junction had to release an Annett's key to free the turntable. A ground frame release to unlock a turntable is a distinct rarity.

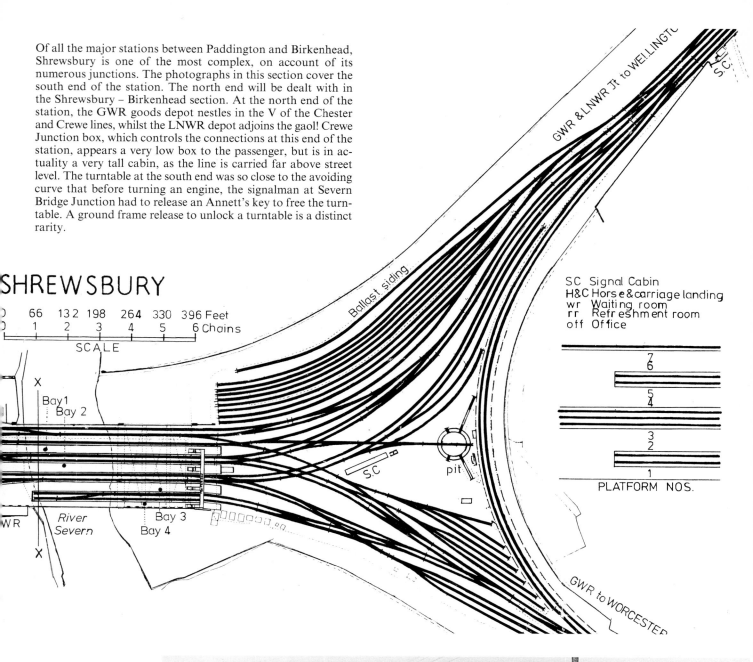

SHREWSBURY

0	66	132	198	264	330	396 Feet
0	1	2	3	4	5	6 Chains

SCALE

SC Signal Cabin
H&C Horse & carriage landing
wr Waiting room
rr Refreshment room
off Office

PLATFORM NOS.

GWR & LNWR Jt to WELLINGTON
S.C.
Ballast siding
S.C
pit
GWR to WORCESTER

Bay 1
Bay 2
River Severn
Bay 3
Bay 4

Severn Bridge Junction box seen from the Hereford curve in 1976, a piece of pure Crewe design in a joint environment.

Branch Lines – The Midlands

Hatton

A plethora of other routes radiated away from the GWR main line between Leamington and Shrewsbury, and if we were to cover all of them, we would weaken the main topic of this book. Therefore, we have neglected the string of long cross country routes which strike south towards Worcester, Kidderminster and Hereford, as these constitute main lines in their own right. Instead we have concentrated on a few lines which are a more integral part of the main line. We begin at Hatton Junction in the summer of 1957, with a non auto-fitted Collett 0-4-2T, No. 5813, still with GWR lettering on the tanks, waiting to depart for Stratford. She was withdrawn that November, a victim of the diesel multiple unit.

Apart from the pretty little 0-4-2Ts, Collett also introduced a range of stylish railcars, some for express, others for branch work. No. W22W of 1940 swings off the Stratford curve at Hatton Junction en route to Leamington in 1956. They always looked very smart, whether in GWR chocolate and cream, or BR red and cream, and it is pleasing that examples have survived into preservation.

Claverdon

Above The Stratford-on-Avon Railway opened as a single track line from Hatton on 10th October 1860. With the creation of the North Warwicks line in 1907-08, the section from Bearley to Stratford was doubled. The Hatton-Bearley portion was not doubled until 2nd July 1938, when the only intermediate station, Claverdon, was completely rebuilt. We see the old station during the change-over.

Below A Riddles 2-8-0, No. 90125, puts out a pall of black smoke as she heads an ironstone train south through Claverdon en route to South Wales in 1957. The old station became a goods store after its replacement by a new station on the south side of the road bridge. Today the line is again single, and Claverdon an unstaffed halt.

Bearley

Above At the next station, Bearley, lines radiated in four directions. The Stratford-on-Avon Railway had opened in 1860, the line to Stratford curving to the left in this view. On 4th September 1876, the independent Alcester Railway opened between Bearley and Alcester, its route curving to the right. With the construction of the North Warwicks line, a triangular junction was established just west of Bearley, which carried direct services from Birmingham to Stratford and Cheltenham. These did not enter the station, but used the third limb of the triangle.

Alcester

Below At Alcester, the single track AR joined the single track Midland Railway branch from Evesham to Redditch, the junction being ¼ mile north of the Midland station. A brick-built shed and water tank were provided for the GWR branch engine. The shed closed in 1915, as a wartime economy, the engine coming instead from Stratford, but on 1st January 1917, the branch closed altogether. It re-opened along with the shed on 1st August 1923. Services were again suspended on 25th September 1939, the branch finally closing in 1951. We see the junction and GWR shed in 1955.

Stratford-on-Avon

Above Leamington's 2-6-2T No. 5192 enters Stratford-on-Avon with the appropriately named "The William Shakespeare" in 1951, providing a through connection from Paddington for those following the track of the bard. The original Stratford-on-Avon terminus of 1860 was near the gas works, and was replaced when a connection was opened in 1861 to the OW&WR branch from Honeybourne. The opening of the North Warwicks line in 1907-08 placed Stratford on the main line between Birmingham and South Wales, via Honeybourne and Gloucester.

Below No. 2812 heads an unfitted class F mineral train, sometimes called an 'up and downer' from its headlamp code, south through Stratford in 1951. As with the Paddington-Birmingham-Birkenhead line, the Birmingham-Stratford-Bristol/South Wales route was a product of competition and railway supremacy, and was doomed to extinction under BR. Express services withered, then locals, and finally, a freight train derailment at Winchcombe in 1976 ended through freight workings.

The North Warwicks Line

The Birmingham & North Warwickshire Railway was initially an independent local venture, authorised in 1894 from a new terminus at Moor St. in Birmingham to Stratford. It was competitive with the GWR who had opposed it, but when the MS&LR, soon to become the Great Central, orchestrated an alliance to provide a GC route between London and Birmingham, the GWR were not amused. The carrot of a GW & GC joint approach to London proved more appealing to the latter and in 1899 the North Warwicks line was revised to run from Tyseley. The GWR took over the following year, and revised the southern end of the line to join the Stratford branch at Bearley. The B&NWR was opened to goods on 9th December 1907 and to passengers on 1st July 1908, trains working into Snow Hill. The GWR saw the North Warwicks as a link in its creation of a Birmingham to Bristol main line, and it was engineered to main line standards, but the string of suburban stations in south Birmingham were to lead to the creation of a modest kind of 'Metroland', with the inner area developing as high grade residential suburbs, and the outer extremity staying fairly rural.

Danzey

Above right Except for the magnificent trees which add a sylvan charm to an otherwise simple station, Danzey for Tanworth had altered little between its opening in 1908 and 1971.

Right Except at the principal stations, economy was the rule, as exemplified by Danzey in 1971.

Grimes Hill

Grimes Hill Platform was another example of economy, as we see from this April 1972 study. The station was renamed Grimes Hill & Wythall in 1914, and is now Wythall.

Hall Green

With the exception of Henley-in-Arden, the southern stations on the North Warwicks line were built as economically as possible, but nearer to Birmingham, the Great Western felt able to spend more freely, and two similar red brick stations were built at Shirley and Hall Green, both of which were to develop as pleasant residential suburbs. At Hall Green the main buildings were on the northbound platform. Some freight was still being handled when this view was taken on 13th January 1964, but today the station is passenger only.

On the southbound platform, the GWR provided a modest brick waiting room at Hall Green, which we see on 15th June 1971. Details which the modeller could emulate include the cables slung along the platform walling, and the odd missing 'tooth' from the ornamental awning.

Tyseley

In another book, one of the authors recounted the story of how he used to visit Southam Road & Harbury station in company with schoolfriends to photograph the last years of GW steam, and of the cry "It's only a Hall", which led to most cameras going down but not the author's! We illustrated a mere 'Hall' at Harbury, truly *Mere Hall* for that is what No. 7915 was named, and add that whilst we might have the laugh there, another of the gang had the laugh on us – he bought a 'Hall' nameplate for a ridiculous price – all of £15. The price would never last – it didn't! When that book came out, we received a delightful letter from that friend, Rodney Wakelin whom we had not seen for many years. What we had not known was that Rodney was seriously ill, and passed away subsequently. We would like the views of Harbury station, and this view – of *Mere Hall* – to stand as a tribute to a Great Western devotee and friend. She is seen heading a children's outing off the North Warwicks line into Tyseley on 1st January 1965.

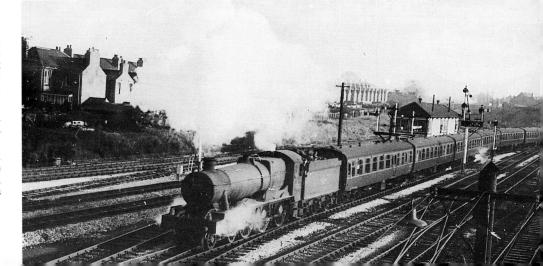

Moor Street

In its independent days, the North Warwicks had planned its own terminus in Birmingham at Moor Street. Under GWR control, the idea was re-examined, for with the growth in suburban traffic, and construction of the GW and GC Joint line and the Bicester cut-off, Snow Hill was not going to be able to cope. The long approach tunnel and the impossibility of enlarging the south end of the station convinced Paddington that a suburban terminal in central Birmingham, which could be reached from the North Warwicks and the main line would be far more cost-effective than any attempt to provide south end bays at Snow Hill. Moor St. opened on 1st July 1909. The station frontage is depicted on 1st June 1971.

Apart from problems over passenger business, the Great Western faced difficulties with freight in Central/South Birmingham. Bordesley, with its viaduct construction, was anything but ideal, and a public goods depot at Moor St. could resolve this problem too. The goods depot opened on 7th January 1914. Its most prominent feature was a commodious two-bay goods warehouse which adjoined the run-round from one of the platforms.

Even before the First World War, land was very costly in central Birmingham, and this had its effect upon Moor St., which for its capacity was on an astonishingly compact site. The example which is commonly given, is that rather than provide run-round crossovers, the three platforms were equipped with traversers. The goods yard was an even more masterly example of space saving. The tracks were cramped together far closer than would normally be acceptable for vehicular access, but this did not matter, for apart from the goods shed, their prime function was to act as sorting roads, for a further set of tracks, reached via a pair of wagon lifts, radiating out underneath the visible trackage! A Class 08 diesel shunts one of the last wagons to use the yard at the start of the 1970s.

Tern Hill

Main lines usually give off branches to left and right, partly to tap traffic, partly as a defensive measure against poaching by rival companies. Between Leamington and Shrewsbury, numerous lines radiated off southwards, but it was not until one reached Wellington that there was a branch to the north. The explanation was simple – the GWR main line came long after the LNWR was well established, and it was totally hemmed in to the north. There were no outlying defences – the Birmingham main line was the front line. North of Wellington the Shropshire/Staffordshire borders lay untapped, and after an abortive attack, which merely served to goad the North Staffordshire Railway into planning a line south-west along the county boundary to Market Drayton, the GWR backed the Nantwich & Market Drayton Railway, which opened in 1863, and the Wellington & Drayton Railway, which was completed in 1867. Local traffic was trivial, but the line gave the GWR access to Crewe. Tern Hill station, immediately south of Market Drayton, is portrayed in September 1963 in the last few days of passenger services.

We could not resist this further view of Tern Hill on account of the superb pagoda. Freight services continued until 1967, but the line is now lifted. The GWR described it as a "very flat and purely agricultural area", and its flatness was to be invaluable in both world wars, as an aerodrome was established at Tern Hill, which contributed considerable traffic to a hitherto sleepy wayside station. In pre-Grouping days, some NSR local trains were allowed to run south of Market Drayton through Tern Hill to Hodnet.

Crewe

Great Western trains ran into Crewe itself, an affront the LNWR must have found hard to swallow! The importance to the GWR of this bit of poaching was access to Crewe with its myriad connections throughout the North, which was invaluable for GWR services via Wellington or on to the Cambrian. No. 7812 *Erlestoke Manor* awaits time at Crewe with a local service.

Shrewsbury to Birkenhead

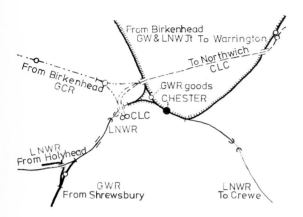

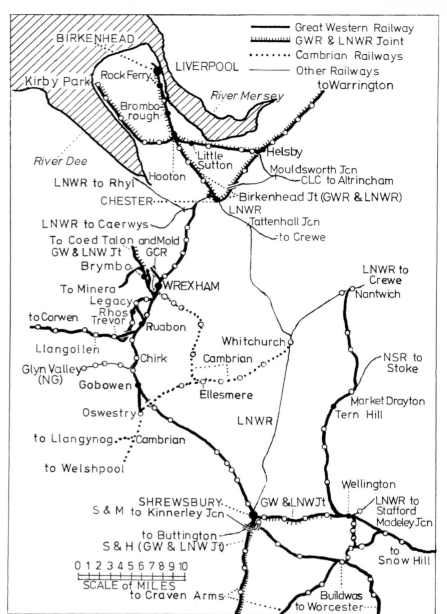

North of Shrewsbury, Great Western trains regained their own metals until Saltney Junction, just over a mile short of Chester, exercising running powers over the LNWR Chester & Holyhead line until the commencement of the GWR & LNWR Birkenhead Joint Railway. Chester was the 'Achilles heel' of the GWR route to the Mersey, for expresses either had to reverse at Chester, or use the avoiding line, and miss the station altogether. Neither option was appealing, and unlike the Midland, which faced a similar problem at Birmingham, and resolved it with a loop line on to the Birmingham & Gloucester line, the GWR were never to overcome this difficulty. Beyond Chester, trains were on the Birkenhead Joint all the way to Birkenhead Woodside. At Woodside, it was only a few yards walk, past the tram and bus terminal to Woodside Ferry, one of several landing stages on the Wirral side of the river. The Mersey ferries maintained a frequent service throughout the day across to Liverpool landing stage, which, with its tram and bus termini, was the heart of Liverpool.

Under BR auspices, there were many changes at Shrewsbury, perhaps the most useful being the remodelling of the south end. Platforms 1 and 2 (alias bays 3 and 4) were resited, and with the resultant space, triple track carried through the station, obviating conflicting moves on platform 3 and the through road. The old mid-platform connection remained however, and the appropriately named No. 1026 *County of Salop* has used it to back on to a long express from the south, the train engine of which is visible in the distance.

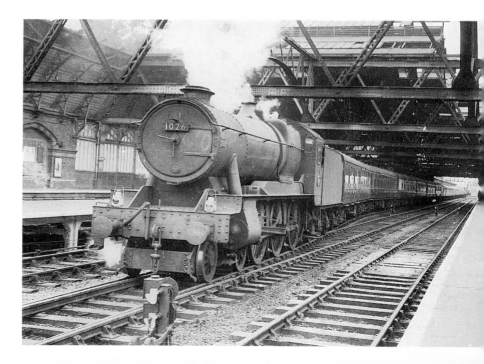

Shrewsbury

A well weathered Old Oak Common 'Castle', No. 7033 *Hartlebury Castle,* takes water from the unusual cantilevered water crane at the north end of Shrewsbury's No. 3 platform in the mid-fifties. As the station was on such a cramped site with residential property nearby, blowing off at the north end of the station frequently led to complaints. Drivers were regularly exhorted to "do everything possible to avoid their engines blowing off excessively".

The signalling at Shrewsbury was a delightful mix of LNWR and GWR, and this gantry, spanning the throat at the north end of the station, is a splendid example of GWR arms, spectacles, finials etc, worked from an LNWR box. As a dmu is signalled in from the Chester line, another move is signalled from the station. The date is 1976, but even today, Shrewsbury retains much of its period charm.

An historic engine, No. 4000 *North Star*, enters Shrewsbury from Chester during the mid-fifties. No. 4000 was built, as No. 40 in 1906, entering service as an Atlantic to permit comparison with the three de Glehn engines bought by Churchward for evaluation. This locomotive proved a striking success, especially after being modified to a 4-6-0 in line with her later sisters. In November 1929 it was totally rebuilt to 'Castle' class standards. In late GWR and early BR days, No. 4000 was a Stafford Road engine, and thus a regular performer on the Chester services, but had moved to Landore prior to her demise in May 1957. In her 51-year career, always as a first line passenger engine, *North Star* ran 2,110,306 miles and whilst quite a number of GWR engines exceeded this life span, none did so as 'Top Link' engines throughout their lives. Although beautifully clean, mechanically she was not so promising by this time, and the Stafford Road men were not averse to her transfer.

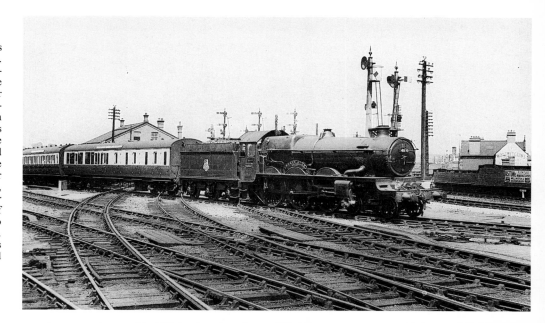

Gobowen

From Shrewsbury, the main line ran north west to the Welsh border, the only community of any size en route being Gobowen, whence a short GWR branch ran as far as Oswestry. The main buildings were on the 'down' platform, and were a perfect example of the Florentine school of architecture. They were of brick construction, with decorative rendering. Windows were mostly round headed, in singles, pairs or triplets, and the station was set off to perfection by a Florentine *campanile* or 'bell' tower which was of Ashlar stone, though this was not apparent, due to the rendering. Thankfully they survived through the fifties and sixties when many fine stations were destroyed, to become a listed building, but were in poor repair. A major restoration, funded by a number of bodies in conjunction with BR, was completed in 1989. Our view, on 25th August 1988 shows the project six months after work had commenced.

We are looking from the level crossing through the platforms towards Shrewsbury. One of the restoration team is on the roof of the 'up' building. The platform canopies were to an uncommon design, and even more surprisingly, separated from the buildings. The Oswestry branch diverged to the right beyond the platforms. The abrupt transition from the level track in the station to a climb of 1 in 165 is apparent.

Looking in the other direction, along the 'down' platform towards Chester, we can study the canopies in more detail – they are more akin to an overgrown 'bike-shed' than the normal GWR canopy. We also see the glorious 'GWR GOBOWEN FOR OSWESTRY' sign. (The quotation marks around GWR are intentional, for this is not an incredible survival, but a welcome departure from corporate image thinking in deference to railway traditionalism. Someone deserves full marks.)

Formerly the general yard was on the 'down' side, adjoining the platform and Oswestry bay, but this had been replaced by a coal depot, with hopper discharge facilities beneath the old run-round, and a conveyor taking coal to a travelling tippler filling a set of hoppers for bagging etc. These two illustrations depict the coal plant for the benefit of modellers.

Bottom right Although the main windows have been modified, Gobowen North Signal Box is a reminder that prior to the mid-1880s, McKenzie & Holland did much work for the GWR. Typical McKenzie features in this box include the semi-round headed window to the locking room, and the tall roof finials. Baschurch and Ruabon were other stations to boast similar McKenzie boxes.

Below Having criticised 'corporate image' signs elsewhere, which use small, lower case lettering, and are difficult to read at any distance or from a moving train, it is pleasant to feature the resurrection of more positive thinking – with this replica GWR sign at Gobowen. It is easy to read, which is what really matters, but it is also elegant.

Ruabon

Ruabon is today a shadow of its former glory, when it was an important junction, for the long route out to Corwen and Barmouth, and the branch loop through Rhos, are long gone, but its Shrewsbury & Chester Railway buildings, this time in the Tudor fashion, survive, although given over to office use. It is amusing that the station should be in stone, for Ruabon was once famous for the very high quality highly-glazed red bricks used in prestige brick buildings.

The Tudor theme shews to good advantage in this study of the exterior of Ruabon buildings, which are approached from a short drive. Of particular interest is the manner in which the corner stones, or quoins, have been finished, with tooling marks sloping alternately to left and right, to produce a 'zig-zag' pattern.

Wrexham

At Wrexham, the original Shrewsbury & Chester Railway station was replaced by a much more commodious single storey GWR structure, seen from the station approach on 25th August 1988. The central feature of the building was a pair of tower-like blocks surmounted by steeply pitched roofs terminating in a flat roof, and owing much to the French chateau style. We have already seen similar buildings at West Drayton and Langley on the old main line out of Paddington. Once more the towers are crowned by exuberant railings.

An overbridge at the south end of Wrexham station provided an excellent vantage point to study the main platforms and the substantial passenger and luggage bridge, with its prominent lift towers. The intermediate ramp on the left-hand loop platform is of interest, and it will be noticed that the rest of the platform is inset from the line. To avoid accidents through a careless passenger not realising there is a gap, the nearer part of the platform is surmounted by the standard spear-tipped railings. The unroofed extension to the footbridge led to the GC Exchange platforms on their line from Connah's Quay to Wrexham Central, where junction was made with the Cambrian Railways.

Victorian engineers were exceptional exponents of ornamental cast iron and steel, as evinced in the fluted columns supporting the canopy on the 'up' platform at Wrexham, and the delicately formed spandrels. The columns are to a very early design, though they could appear quite late on (as at Weston-super-Mare in the 1880s). The concertina door to the luggage lift is visible at the end of the 'arcade'.

Looking south from platform 2 at Wrexham General in August 1988. The canopy is quite different to the much older structure on platform 1. The south end bays on the 'up' side are visible beyond the road overbridge.

LMS & GW INTERNAL CORRESPONDENCE.	Our Reference.	Your Reference.

TO Signalmen No.5.Box.

From Station Master

AT Chester

(Centre No.).   Extn.   (Centre No.

E.R.O. 70014

I.3.39 _____ 19

ANNUAL LEAVE. 1939

Your Annual Leave has been arranged as follows :-

Beavan   T.G. April   17th to April   22nd.
Dorricott   A.   June   5th - June   10th.
Thomas   R.   September 25th - Septembr 30th. as Oct.

for A.E.Mawson.

Chester

With electrification on the LNWR route, through services from Paddington to Birkenhead last ra on Saturday 4th March 1967. To commemora the occasion a special train was arranged by Ia Allan, using an old GWR name "The Zulu" Diesel-hauled as far as Banbury, No. 7029 *Ch Castle* took over for the run to Birkenhead. Sh is portrayed at the west end of Chester Genera station, during the complicated shunt moves re quired.

Staff at Chester came under the auspices of th Chester & Birkenhead Section, so that "LMS GW" stationery was the order of the day.

Chester General station in 1964, looking towar Crewe on the LMS and Helsby and Warringto section of the GW and LMS Joint.

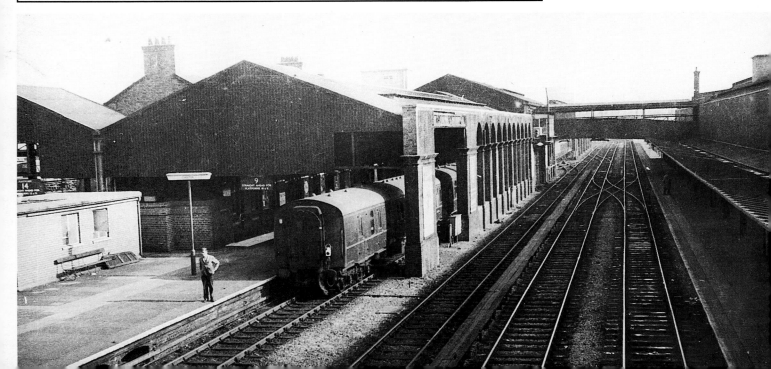

Hooton Junction

its prime, the Birkenhead Joint carried an im-
nse traffic, and was quadrupled from Ledsham,
miles north of Chester, to Birkenhead (Green
ne Junction). At Hooton, two miles north of
dsham, the main line was joined by two trail-
junctions, from West Kirby to the west, and
lsby to the east. We have a signalman's eye view
m the South box on 29th March 1971, as 2-car
u, headed by a Metro-Cam driving trailer com-
. No. M56348 heads towards Chester on the 'up'
w. A Class 47 is waiting in the 'down' slow plat-
m, and a further train is signalled from the bay
the right hand side of the picture for Little Sut-
and Helsby. Today, much of the trackage has
e. Merseyside electric units now work out to
ooton, rather than Rock Ferry, and passengers
ange trains for Chester.

Bromborough

omborough station was located 1½ miles north
Hooton. In March 1971, it still possessed all four
cks.

Rock Ferry

om 1891, the Chester & Birkenhead Railway
de connections with the Mersey Railway at
ck Ferry. Originally steam worked, the Mersey
s electrified in 1903, and remained independent
til 1948, although working closely with the LMS
ich electrified its Wirral lines in the thirties.
ssengers who did not fancy the ferry trip, could
nsfer to the Mersey Railway for the run to Liver-
ol Central (Low Level). An LMS-designed, Wir-
3-car set sits in the Mersey Railway bays at
ck Ferry in 1982. The bays, although only
d by the Mersey Railway, were LMS & GW
nt property!

Birkenhead Woodside

Above No. 5153, a 2-6-2T makes an impressive start away from Birkenhead (Woodside), with a Great Western local in April 1930, as one of Birkenhead's 2021 class open cab panniers blows off in the adjacent platform. The cramped nature of the station is clear, No. 1 platform being but 537 feet overall. Clearances were also tight, and 73ft GWR stock was not to stand on the curved portion of No. 3 siding.

Below The crew of 'Barnum' class 4-4-0 No. 3216 pose somewhat self-consciously with their steed at Woodside in April 1930. When fitted with a larger boiler at Wolverhampton in 1899, Stafford Road had felt it necessary to increase the height of the cab with a unique modification – increasing the depth of the sidesheets above the cut-out.

Above As well as providing a good study of the sharply curved station site and two roof spans, we are reminded of the LNWR and LMS presence in this 1930 portrait of a Bowen Cooke 4-6-2T, No. 6975 blowing off in the centre road. Woodside station was opened on 1st April 1878, and closed to passengers on 5th November 1967.

Below No. 3580, one of the ten 3571 class 0-4-2Ts, which were developed from the 517 class, pauses with a 'Toplight' coach at Woodside in 1930. Dating from January 1897, this was the last of the class to carry the Dean type boiler with raised, round-topped firebox, not receiving a Belpaire boiler until 1934.

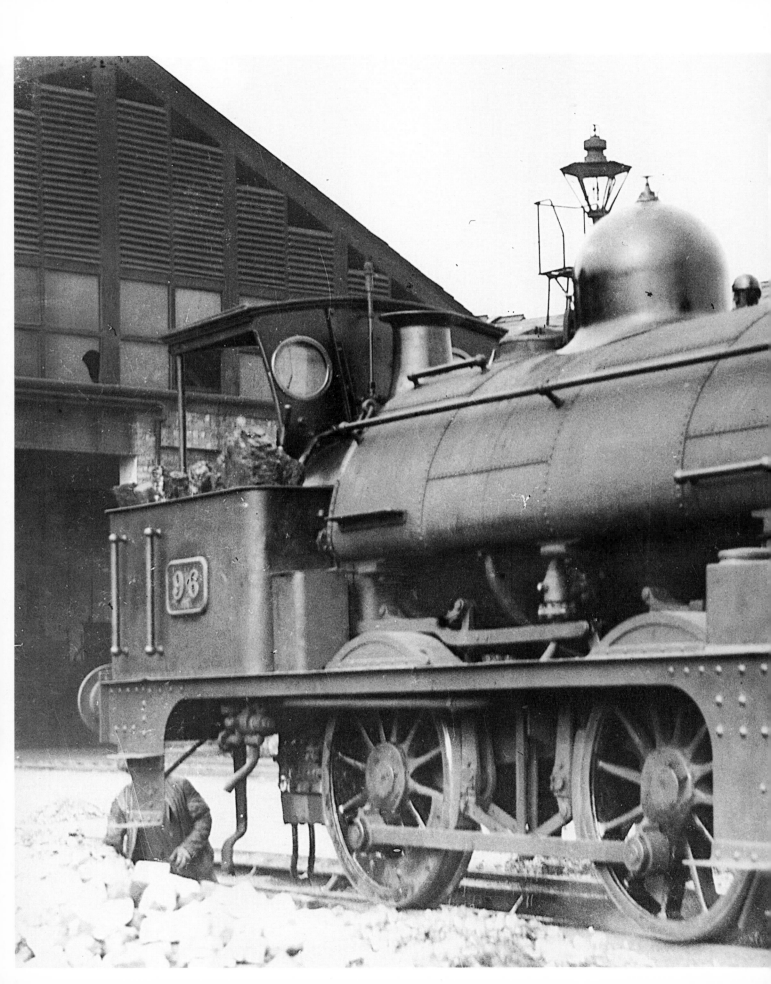

Birkenhead Docks

It is seldom in any book on the Great Western that a humble 0-4-0 saddle tank is accorded 'star' status, but if any engine deserves it, then No. 96 does, for as we look at her, we see an engine which was in use at the dawn of the 'narrow gauge' era on the GWR.

When the Chester & Birkenhead Railway opened on 23rd September 1840, Birkenhead was still a small community on the Wirral bank of the Mersey. Plans were afoot for a dock system, but it was not until the mid-forties, that this began to take shape. The railway started life with the typical engines of the day, 2-2-2 tender locomotives, adding 2-4-0s and 0-4-2s in due course. In 1854, the company acquired a secondhand 0-4-0T for shunting, and in 1856-57 a pair of slightly larger 0-4-0 saddle tanks from Sharp, Stewart. In 1860, the Birkenhead Railway was taken over jointly by the GWR and LNWR, and the two Sharp, Stewart tanks allocated to the GWR, as Nos 95 and 96. Some doubt has always existed as to which engine received which number, but the accepted version is that the 1856 engine, No. 39 *Cricket,* became GWR No. 96.

This locomotive received a major rebuild at Wolverhampton in 1888 and remained in service, with her 1888 boiler, until November 1935, spending virtually the whole of her career in the Northern Division.

This portrait, from a negative in the authors' collection taken by the late J. N. Maskelyne, shews No. 96 at Wolverhampton, probably in 1922. Instead of a conventional front coupling hook and links, it has an eye bolt and shackle, an archaic arrangement, which was frowned upon for wagons before the turn of the century! Although fitted with sprung buffers at the rear, she lacks such a refinement at the front. From another Maskelyne photograph it seems that she may have run in this form at some stage, which could scarcely have been good for fragile goods!

It is a strange thought that No. 96 was shunting the Birkenhead Docks 130 years ago, yet survived – just – into the dawn of the diesel age, for by her demise in 1935, the first seven GWR diesel railcars were running.

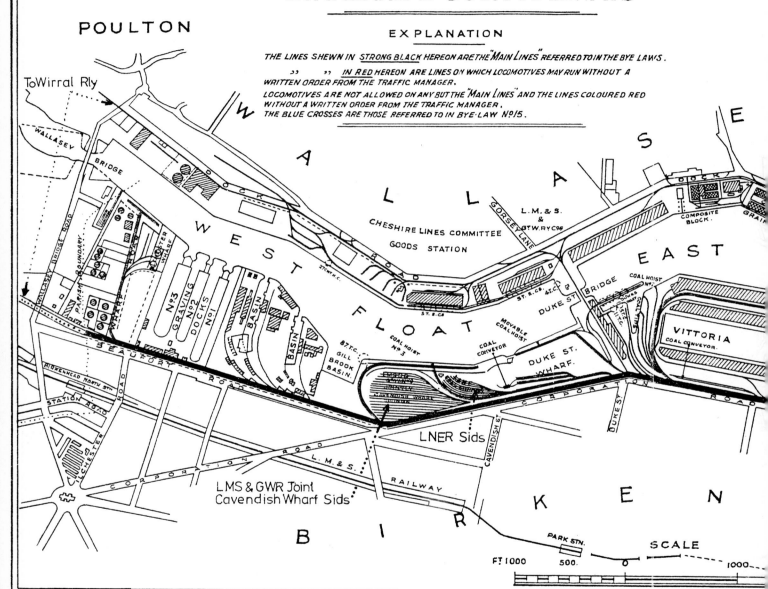

Birkenhead Dock

Although the Birkenhead Dock Railways were largely owned by the Mersey Docks & Harbour Board (later 'Company'), the dock railways form such an integral part of the route from Paddington to the Mersey that they must be included if the story is to make sense. In contrast to most ports, which comprise a series of docks along the banks of the navigable waterway, the Birkenhead docks run inland for two miles. At their widest point, their frontage to the Mersey, they occupy no more than 1,000 yards. This curious configuration arose through use of the Wallasey Pool, a tidal inlet between Birkenhead and Wallasey. By the 1820s, before the railway age had dawned, Liverpool was already a massive port with 46 acres of Docks, and it was not for another twenty years that there was to be any progress in the Wirral. When it came, it was under the auspices of the independent Birkenhead Dock Co. which secured Parliamentary powers in 1844, and by 1847 the Egerton and Morpeth Docks were open, but over-spending and mismanagement brought the company to its knees, and in 1858 it was incorporated into the new Mersey Docks & Harbour Board, and came under the guidance of the brilliant Liverpool docks engineer, Jesse Hartley.

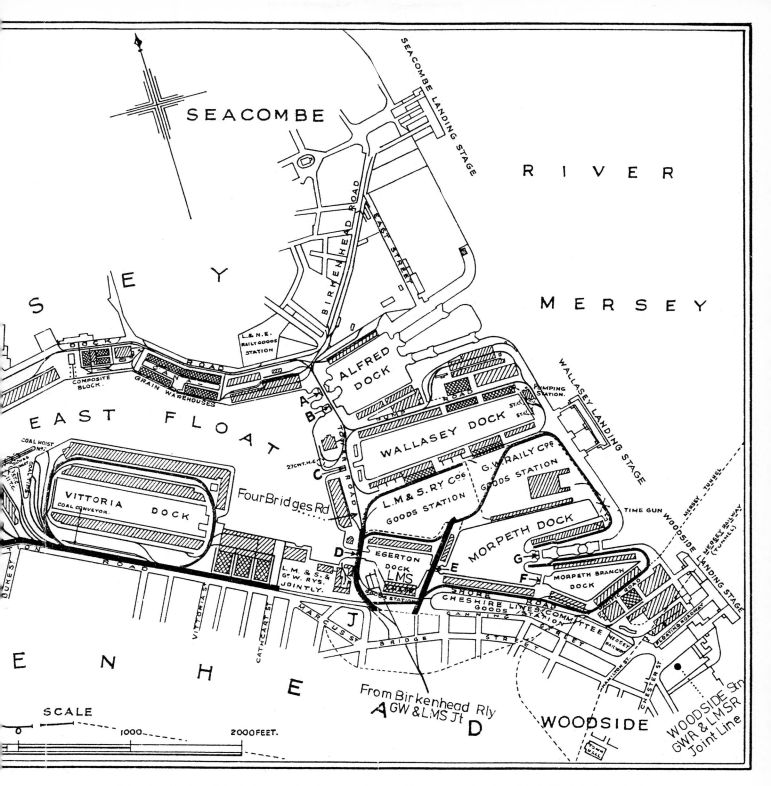

The original for this plan of the docks was printed in two colours and issued in conjunction with the Dock Railways byelaws between the wars. It shows the docks at their peak. On the original, the main lines of the MDHB are shewn in thick black, secondary lines are in a medium thickness red (which reproduces as a medium black line) and MDHB sidings *and* running lines of the LMS or GWR are shewn in fine black lines. This is at first confusing, but with a little study, becomes obvious. The junction to and from the Birkenhead Joint is at Canning St., 'J' on the map. The section of thin line from Canning St. to Cathcart St. is GW and LMS property.

At its western extremity, just beyond No. 3 Graving Dock (which comes off the West Float), an end-on junction is made with the Wirral section of the LMS. MDHB lines reach the northern or Wallasey bank via the Duke St. bridge, and the "Four Bridges" route, so called on account of its four bridges, marked A, B, C and D on the plan. A network of lines exist on the north bank, and at the western end, near Poulton, make a connection with the Wirral Railway. Woodside passenger station, not shewn on the plan as such, was between Chester St. and Woodside landing stage.

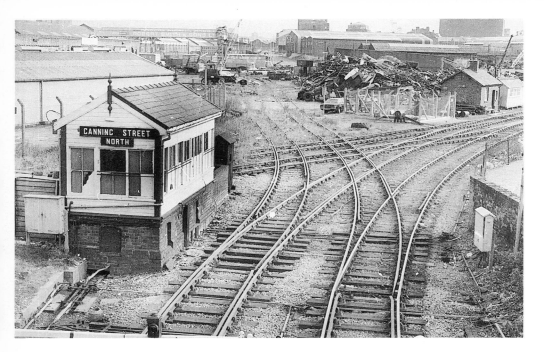

The extraordinary complexity of the dock railways is revealed in this portrait of Canning Street North on 8th October 1982, with its 'double scissors' junction. The lines vanishing behind the box are from the Four Bridges route, and are one of the MDHB 'main lines'. They gave access to the north face of the East Float, the Alfred and Wallasey Docks and the LMS and GWR goods depots. The lines heading off to the centre of the view, with connections from the Four Bridges line, and from the tracks in the foreground, were the MDHB secondary line to Morpeth Dock, but at the time of writing only served Robert Smith & Sons scrap yard. The line vanishing to the right, is the LMS and GW line to Blackpool St. and the Birkenhead Joint. The foreground tracks pass over Tower Road level crossing en route to the Vittoria Dock and West Float. Block working was in force between Canning St. and Blackpool St., but not westwards over the MDHB lines.

We are looking west in October 1982 from the Tower Road level crossing footbridge at Canning St. towards the West Float. The actual hand-over point between the GW & LMS Joint and the MDHB was at Cathcart St. Just beyond the occupation crossing, there is a low brick wall, which becomes suddenly much taller, towards the centre of the photograph. This defines the hand-over point. The nest of four sidings on the right occupy the site of structures demolished since the date of the plan on pages 122/3.

Dock railways always abound with sharp curves and awkward places to work, hence the need for diminutive shunting engines such as No. 96. Private sidings are amongst the worst of these. This horrifying curve served premises on Tower Road, between the level crossing previously referred to and bridge 'D', a distance of little more than 100 yards! The granite sets were typical of the dock roads of byegone days.

The area around 'C' bridge on the Four Bridges route was one of the most interesting in the dock system. By 1982, this route was out of use, but sufficient remains to recapture the character of this extraordinary area. In the foreground, we have 'C' bridge itself, a balanced lift bridge, controlled from the wooden control room spanning the road. 'C' bridge spanned the entrance from the East Float to Wallasey Dock, which was opened in 1863. On the extreme right are the warehouses between Wallasey Dock and Alfred Dock, the bows of a vessel in the latter dock being just visible. Through the girders of 'C' bridge can be seen the two bridges between the East Float and Alfred Dock, one a lift bridge, the other a swing bridge. Immediately to the left of 'C' bridge control tower is Jesse Hartley's 1863 Campanile Hydraulic Tower. In the days before electricity, it would have been too costly to use steam for all powered appliances in the docks area, so Hartley developed a hydraulic power system, of which the Campanile tower was the hub.

Although the MDHB operated a sizeable fleet of steam locomotives in the Liverpool docks, shunting on the Wirral side was farmed out to the railway companies and certain private owners, all of whom worked under MDHB byelaws. The railways required small steam locomotives such as No. 96. When steam was phased out, BR Class 03 0-6-0 diesel shunters filled the gap, for with their light axleload, and ability to negotiate tight curves, they were ideal. No. 03170 pauses between shunting moves between Vittoria Dock and Duke St. on 8th October 1982. By the summer of 1988, Birkenhead had become the last mainland refuge for the 03 shunter on BR, finally being withdrawn in March 1989.

With a Polish vessel at the Duke St. Wharf on the East Float as a backdrop, No. 03170 awaits her next move in October 1982. The tracks to the left lead to Duke St. yard, Cavendish Wharf, and eventually the Wirral Railway and Birkenhead North.

Birkenhead Ferry

The ferry service between Birkenhead and Liverpool dates back at least to the days of King Edward III so, by several centuries, is the most historic part of the whole journey. Municipal interest began in the 1840s, and continued until the formation of the Merseyside PTE in 1969. The former Wallasey ferry, TSMV *Royal Iris* of 1950, and the Birkenhead ferry, TSMV *Mountwood* of 1960 are alongside Woodside landing stage on 30th April 1985.

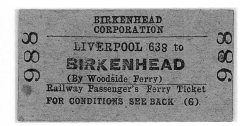

Above Railway passengers qualified for special cheap through fares on the Woodside ferry, and one of the special Birkenhead Corporation tickets is shown.

Liverpool (Pier Head)

Merseyside's darling, the legendary *Royal Iris* is at the Liverpool landing stage. Pier Head bus terminal lies at the head of the ramps. Beyond that is the equally celebrated Liver Building, with its mythical Liver Birds. To the traveller by the Great Western route, or seafarer from across the globe, it heralds Journey's End.

Liverpool (James Street)

The GWR maintained its own freight office in central Liverpool, as recalled by this May 1875 waybill to Audlem.

(111)

GREAT WESTERN RAILWAY.

Parcels' Way Bill, No. _____ LIVERPOOL (11, James St.) to _____

_____ o'clock Train, _____ 187 _

FREDERICK BELL & Co., "Imperial Works," Chelsea.

No. of Parcel.	Description.	NAME.	ADDRESS.	Weight Lbs.	Paid Through £ s. d.	Paid on. £ s. d.	Paid. £ s. d.	To Pay. £ s. d.	Remarks.
1									
2									
3									
4									
5									
6									

BIRKENHEAD AND CHESTER.

Week Days.

	a.m.	a.m.	a.m.	a.m.	a.m.	a.m.	a.m.	a.m.	a.m.	a.m.	a.m.	a.m.	a.m.	a.m.	a.m.	a.m.
BIRKENHEAD Woodside dep.	5 0	5 30	5 50	6 15	6 25	6 30	7 3	7 8	7 25	7 35	7 55	8 0	8 20	8 30	9 20	10 5
BIRKENHEAD Town ... "	...	...	...	...	6 28	6 33	7 6	...	7 28	7 38	...	...	...	...	...	...
Rock Ferry "	5 7	5 38	5 56	6 22	6 35	6 42	7 13	7 17	7 34	7 44	8 5	8 6	8 26	8 40	9 27	10 13
Bebington and New Ferry ... "	5 9	...	...	...	6 38	6 45	7 16	7 20	7 37	7 47	8 8	...	8 30	...	...	10 16
Port Sunlight "	5 12	5 42	6 1	6 27	6 42	6 49	7 20	.	7 41	7 51	8 14	...	8 33	...	9 33	...
Spital "	...	...	...	...	...	6 52	7 23	...	7 44	7 54	8 17	.	8 36	.	9 36	.
Bromborough "	.	.	6 6	...	6 48	6 57	7 28	7 27	7 49	7 59	8 22	...	8 40	...	9 40	10 21
Hooton "	5 20	5 50	6 14	6 35	6 53	7 6	7 34	7 33	7 54	8 4	8 27	8 19	8 45	8 52	9 47	10 27
Ledsham "	—	—	.	—	—	.	—	7 37	—	—	—	8 21	—	.	.	—
Capenhurst "	...	...	6 22	...	...	7 13	...	7 44	...	...	...	8 27	...	...	...	...
Mollington "	.	.	.	.	.	7 18	.	7 48	.	.	.	8 31	.	.	.	.
Upton-by-Chester Halt "	...	...	...	...	...	7 23	...	...	...	...	...	8 35	...	...	...	...
CHESTER (General) arr.	.	.	6 31	.	.	7 33	.	7 55	.	.	.	8 40	.	9 4	10 2	.

	a.m.	a.m.	a.m.	p.m.	p.m.	p.m.	p.m.	p.m.	p.m.	p.m.	p.m.	p.m.	p.m.	p.m.	p.m.	p.m.
BIRKENHEAD Woodside dep.	10 30	.	11 35	.	.	12G25	12S30	12 36	12 45	.	.	1S20	1S30	1 35	1S48	2G 5
BIRKENHEAD Town ... "	...	...	...	...	③	...	...	12 38	...	③	...	...	1S32	1 37	...	...
Rock Ferry "	10 37	11S25	11 44	12S 4	12 25	12G36	12S36	12 45	12 51	1G15	1S20	1S26	1S37	1 47	1S53	2G13
Bebington and New Ferry ... "	10 44	11S27	...	12S 8	12 27	...	...	12 47	12 54	1G17	1S22	...	1S42	1 49	...	2G15
Port Sunlight "	10 50	11S30	.	...	12 30	...	12S43	12 50	.	1G20	1S25	.	.	1 55	.	2G18
Spital "	10 55	11S32	...	12S12	12 32	...	...	12 52	...	1G22	1S27	...	...	1 57	.	2G20
Bromborough "	10 59	11S36	.	12S16	12 36	.	.	12 56	.	1G26	1S31	.	1S48	2 1	.	2G24
Hooton "	11 7	11S41	11 55	12S23	12 41	12G46	12S52	1 1	1 3	1G31	1S36	1S40	1S53	2 9	2S 5	2G29
Ledsham "	11 9	—	.	—	—	.	.	—	—	—	—	1S42	—	2 12	—	—
Capenhurst "	11 13	...	...	...	...	...	12S58	...	...	...	...	...	...	2 17	...	...
Mollington "	11 17	.	.	...	.	.	.	.	.	.	.	.	.	2 21	.	.
Upton-by-Chester Halt "	11 21	.	.	...	.	.	.	.	.	.	.	.	.	2 25	.	.
CHESTER (General) arr.	11 26	.	12 8	.	.	1G 2	1S 7	.	.	.	.	1S55	.	2 32	.	.

	p.m.	p.m.	p.m.	p.m.	p.m.	p.m.	p.m.	p.m.	p.m.	p.m.	p.m.	p.m.	p.m.	p.m.	p.m.	p.m.	p.m.	p.m.	p.m.
BIRKENHEAD Woodside dep.	2 35	3G 5	3S13	3S30	4 5	4 20	4 25	4 35	③	5G 5	5 15	5G20	5 35	5G40	5 48	6 5	6 10	6S20	6G20
BIRKENHEAD Town ... "	...	3G 7	3S15	...	4 7	...	...	4S37	...	...	...	...	...	...	5 51	...	6 13	...	...
Rock Ferry "	2 43	3G16	3S22	3S37	4 14	4K26	4 34	4 43	5G 1	5G11	5 26	5G26	5 41	5G51	6 1	6 11	6 16	6S26	6G26
Bebington and New Ferry "	...	3G18	3S24	...	4 16	—	...	4 45	5G 3	...	5 30	...	...	...	6 5	...	6 23	...	...
Port Sunlight "	.	3G23	3S27	.	4 19	Through Carriages to ☞ London (Padd.)	.	4 48	5G 6	.	5 34	.	5 48	.	6 9	.	6 27	.	.
Spital "	...	3G25	3S29	...	4 22		...	4 51	5G 9	...	5 37	...	...	...	6 12	...	6 31	...	...
Bromborough "	.	3G29	3S33	.	4 26		.	4 55	5G13	.	5 42	5G35	.	5G57	6 17	.	6 36	.	.
Hooton "	2 53	3G39	3S39	3S50	4 31		4 44	5 6	5G18	5G23	5 48	5G43	5 58	6G 2	6 23	6 24	6 41	6S40	6G40
Ledsham "	.	.	—	.	—		.	5 8	—	.	—	.	.	—	6 29	—	—	.	.
Capenhurst "	...	3G45	...	3S56	...		...	5 13	...	...	...	5G50	...	...	6 37	...	...	...	...
Mollington "	.	.	.	.	.		.	5 17	.	.	.	5G55	.	.	6 42	.	.	6S50	6G50
Upton-by-Chester Halt "	...	...	...	...	...		...	5 21	...	...	...	6G 0	...	...	6 47	...	...	...	6G56
CHESTER (General) arr.	3 5	3G54	.	4S 8	.		5 2	5 26	.	5G36	.	6G 5	6 11	.	6 52	.	.	6S57	7G 3

	p.m.	p.m.	p.m.	p.m.	p.m.	p.m.	p.m.	p.m.
BIRKENHEAD Woodside dep	.	7 0	7 35	8 10	8 35	8 55	10 10	11 10
BIRKENHEAD Town ... "	...	7 3	...	8 13	...	...	...	...
Rock Ferry "	6S35	7 11	7 44	8 21	8 44	9 5	10 17	11 23
Bebington and New Ferry ... "	6S38	7 14	...	8 24	8 47	...	10 21	11 27
Port Sunlight "	6S45	7 18	.	8 28	8 51	.	10 25	.
Spital "	6S49	7 21	...	8 31	8 55	...	10 28	11 32
Bromborough "	6S54	7 26	.	8 36	9 0	.	10 33	11 38
Hooton "	7S 3	7 31	7 54	8 41	9 10	9 19	10 42	11 46
Ledsham "	7S 6	—	7 56	—	.	9 22	10 45	.
Capenhurst "	7S14	...	8 1	...	...	9 28	10 50	...
Mollington "	7S19	.	8 5	.	.	9 33	10 54	.
Upton-by-Chester Halt "	...	...	8 9	...	...	9 38	...	...
CHESTER (General) arr.	7S31	.	8 14	.	9 26	9 44	11 1	11 58

THE WHOLE OF THE TRAIN, STEAMER AND ROAD SERVICES, ALSO SLEEPING CARS, SHEWN IN THIS TIME TABLE ARE SUBJECT TO ALTERATION OR CANCELLATION AT SHORT NOTICE.

Sundays.

	a.m.	a.m.	a.m.	a.m.	a.m.	p.m.	p.m.	p.m.	p.m.	p.m.	p.m.	p.m.	p.m.	p.m.	p.m.
BIRKENHEAD Woodside dep.	7 10	7 40	8 15	8 45	10 15	2 0	2 55	3 20	4 45	5 0	6 40	7 45	8 5	8 50	9 53
BIRKENHEAD Town ... "	...	...	...	...	...	...	...	...	...	...	...	...	...	...	...
Rock Ferry "	7 20	7 48	8 22	8 53	10 23	2 8	3 0	3 28	4 53	5 8	6 50	7 55	8 15	8 58	10 1
Bebington and New Ferry ... "	...	7 50	8 24	8 55	10 25	2 10	...	3 30	4 55	...	...	7 58	...	9 1	10 5
Port Sunlight "	7 27	7 53	8 27	8 58	10 28	2 13	.	3 33	4 58	.	.	8 4	.	9 5	10 9
Spital "	7 30	7 55	8 29	9 0	10 30	2 15	...	3 35	5 0	...	...	8 7	...	9 8	10 12
Bromborough "	7 35	7 59	8 33	9 4	10 34	2 19	.	3 39	5 4	.	.	8 12	8 22	9 13	10 17
Hooton "	7 44	8 4	8 38	9 11	10 41	2 26	3 15	3 44	5 11	5 16	7 1	8 20	8 27	9 22	10 25
Ledsham "	.	—	—	9 14	10 43	2 29	.	—	5 14	—	.	8 23	—	9 25	10 28
Capenhurst "	...	...	...	9 19	10 48	2 35	...	...	5 19	...	...	8 29	...	9 31	10 34
Mollington "	7 56	.	.	9 23	10 52	2 40	.	.	5 23	.	.	8 34	.	9 36	10 39
Upton-by-Chester Halt "	...	...	...	9 27	10 56	2 44	...	...	5 27	...	...	8 39	...	...	...
CHESTER (General) arr.	8 4	.	.	9 32	11 1	2 49	3 27	.	5 32	.	7 13	8 44	.	9 44	10 48

HOOTON AND HELSBY.

Week Days. / **Sundays**

	a.m.	a.m.	a.m.	a.m.	a.m.	a.m.	a.m.	p.m.	p.m.	p.m.	p.m.	p.m.	p.m.	p.m.	p.m.	p.m.	p.m.	p.m.	p.m.	p.m.	Sun. a.m.	Sun. p.m.
Hooton ...... dep.	5 24	6 56	7 36	8 7	8 33	8 53	11S42	1 2	2S12	3G 5	3S43	3G58	4G35	5 5	5S25	6G 5	6 44	7 32	8 44	10 45	8 9	5 18
Little Sutton "	5 28	7 1	7 40	8 11	8 37	8 57	11S49	1 9	2S16	3G 9	3S47	4G 2	4G39	5 9	5S29	6G 9	6 48	7 39	8 49	10 50	8 13	5 22
Ellesmere Port ... "	5 34	7 10	7 46	8 17	8 43	9 3	11S55	1 18	2S21	3G14	3S53	4G 8	4G44	5 14	5S34	6G14	6 54	7 45	8 55	10 56	8 20	5 28
Stanlow & Thornton "	5 41	7 20	7 55	8 23	8 49	.	12S 2	1 24	.	3G20	3S59	4G14	.	5 20	5S41	6G22	.	7 52	9 2	.	8 26	5 34
Ince and Elton ... "	5 45	7 26	7 59	8 26	—	9 9	12S 6	1 27	2S27	3G23	4S 2	4G17	4G50	5 23	5S44	6G25	7 2	7 56	9 6	11 3	8 29	5 37
Helsby . . arr.	5 50	7 31	8 4	8 31	.	9 14	12S10	1 32	2S32	3G28	4S 7	4G22	4G55	5 28	5S49	6G30	7 7	8 1	9 11	11 8	8 34	5 42

	a.m.	a.m.	a.m.	a.m.	a.m.	a.m.	a.m.	a.m.	p.m.	p.m.	p.m.	p.m.	p.m.	p.m.	p.m.	p.m.	p.m.	p.m.	p.m.	p.m.	Sun. a.m.	Sun. p.m.
Helsby ...... dep.	6 10	6 35	7 37	8 10	8 41	...	10 0	...	12S25	2 10	2S50	3G55	4S40	4G50	5G15	6 26	7 25	8 17	10 0	11S20	9 30	6 5
Ince and Elton . "	6 14	6 38	7 40	8 13	8 44	.	10 3	11S32	12S29	2 14	2S53	3G58	4S43	4G54	5G20	6 31	7 29	8 24	10 4	.	9 33	6 9
Stanlow & Thornton "	6 19	6 43	7 45	8 18	8 48	9 3	10 7	...	12S39	2 19	2S57	4G 2	4S47	...	5G25	6 35	7 34	8 29	10§17	...	9 37	6 19
Ellesmere Port . . "	6 26	6 50	7 52	8 25	8 55	9 9	10 14	11S38	12S46	2 25	3S 3	4G 8	4S53	5G 4	5G35	6 45	7 41	8 36	10 24	11S28	9 43	6 26
Little Sutton ... "	6 32	6 55	7 58	8 31	9 0	9 14	10 19	11S43	12S51	2 30	3S 8	4G13	4S58	5G10	5G41	6 50	7 47	8 42	10 30	11S33	9 48	6 32
Hooton . . arr.	6 37	7 1	8 3	8 36	9 5	9 19	10 24	11S48	12S56	2 35	3S13	4G19	5S 3	5G15	5G46	6 55	7 52	8 47	10 35	11S39	9 53	6 37

BIRKENHEAD AND LIVERPOOL. (WOODSIDE FERRY PASSENGER SERVICE.)

Single Fare 2d.—(9d. for night boat between 12.35 a.m. and 4.0 a.m., inclusive).

BIRKENHEAD (Woodside) TO LIVERPOOL (Landing Stage).

MONDAYS TO FRIDAYS:—12.15 a.m., 12.50, 1.30, 2.30, 3.30, 4.30, 5.15 5.45, 6.15, 6.45, 7.0, then every 10 minutes, 7.0 a.m. to 10.0 a.m., ½ hourly 10.0 a.m. to 4.0 p.m., every 10 minutes 4.0 p.m. to 7.0 p.m., ½ hourly 7.0 p.m. to 10.45 p.m., 11.15 and 11.45 p.m.

SATURDAYS:—As above till 12.0 noon, every 10 minutes 12.0 noon to 4.0 p.m., ½ hourly 4.0 p.m. to 10.45 p.m., 11.15 and 11.45 p.m.

SUNDAYS:—As above till 7.0 a.m., every 10 minutes 7.0 a.m. to 8.0 a.m., ½ hourly 8.0 a.m. to 10.45 p.m., 11.15 and 11.45 p.m.

LIVERPOOL (Landing Stage) TO BIRKENHEAD (Woodside).

MONDAYS TO FRIDAYS:—12.0 midnight, 12.35 a.m., 1.5, 2.0, 3.0, 4.0, 5.0, 5.30, 6.0, 6.30, 7.0, then every 10 minutes 7.0. a.m. to 10.0 a.m., ½ hourly 10.0 a.m. to 4.0 p.m., every 10 minutes 4.0 p.m. to 7.0 p.m., ½ hourly 7.0 p.m. to 10.30 p.m.; 11.0 and 11.30 p.m.

SATURDAYS:—As above till 12.0 noon, every 10 minutes 12.0 noon to 4.0 p.m., ½ hourly 4.0 p.m. to 10.30 p.m., 11.0 and 11.30 p.m.

SUNDAYS:—As above till 7.0 a.m., every 10 minutes 7.0 a.m. to 8.0 a.m., ½ hourly 8.0 a.m. to 10.30 p.m., 11.0 and 11.30 p.m.

G—Saturdays excepted. K—Calls to pick up passengers only. S—Saturdays only. §—Arrive 10.8 p.m. ③—Third class only.

Branch Lines – The North

North of Shrewsbury, Wolverhampton Division branches fell into three types. There was a 53¾ mile line to Barmouth and the Cambrian, the extremity of which was in the Oswestry Division. Next, there were the short lines around Ruabon and Wrexham catering for minerals, and finally the secondary routes of the Birkenhead Joint Railway.

Ruabon

Right The Barmouth branch and its connections tapped virtually every significant community for 50 miles, as the sign at Ruabon reveals.

Rhos

Right The Rhos loop and the spurs around Brymbo served lime kilns, brick works, collieries and the iron industry. Sharp curves, severe grades and 'yellow' route restriction made operation difficult. The Rhos branch lost its passenger workings in 1931, so was an obvious choice for an early SLS/MLS railtour on 6th September 1952. Autofitted pannier No. 6405 takes water at Rhos.

Corwen

Opposite top Corwen, 15½ miles west of Ruabon, on the Barmouth branch, was a sizeable community for the area, and was the junction for the LNWR branch from Denbigh and Rhyl. East Box, on the 'up' platform, controlled the junction, and the three levers pulled, 4, 5 and 6 indicate a train is signalled from the LMS.

Barmouth Junction

Opposite below Barmouth Junction, although a part of the Oswestry Division, is a more realistic end-point for this necessarily brief diversion along the Corwen branch than the actual division point, which used to be 30 chains west of Dolgelly station. "Dukedog" 4-4-0 No. 9018 pauses with a local from Corwen and Dolgelly to Barmouth in the early fifties. Other than for the savage dent in the dome cover, No. 9018 is well groomed.

Brymbo

Right The Brymbo branch, which had also lost its passenger services, was another line explored by the Denbighshire rail tour. As we look towards Wrexham, enthusiasts fan out to take photographs. A participant on the trip recalls that an ice-cream van, which chanced to be at the nearby level crossing, did a roaring trade. At Brymbo the lines split, one line going to Minera, the other, LMS & GW c' it, heading for Mold.

Little Sutton

The construction of a 'cut-off' from Hooton to Helsby Junction in 1863 provided a direct link between the industrial heartlands of Lancashire and the Birkenhead Docks, and gave the Great Western an improbable foothold on this important traffic. The stations, with their dark rough-hewn rustic stone and Tudor or Jacobean motif, were as typical of the northern lines, as they were atypical of the Great Western. Little Sutton, seen in 1971, would have looked more at home on the Lancaster & Carlisle or the 'Long Drag' than with GWR engines and stock!

Helsby

At Helsby, the Hooton branch made connection with the Cheshire Lines Committee branch from Mouldsworth and Northwich, and with the main Birkenhead Joint line between Chester and Walton Junction on the outskirts of Warrington. The GWR possessed running powers from Warrington to Manchester (Exchange). The main buildings at Helsby were executed in Jacobean style, using a dark rock-faced sandstone, and were pleasingly different to Little Sutton. The wooden building to the left is pure LNWR, to a design introduced from 1880 onwards for general purpose huts, mess rooms etc.

The signal cabin at Helsby was another example of LNWR design, and with the North Western wooden cabin on the right, gives the station a strongly LNWR look. The station handled a heavy through traffic, but for terminating passenger services ex-Hooton, was limited to not more than six bogie coaches.

LOCAL INSTRUCTIONS, CHESTER AND BIRKENHEAD SECTION.

Birkenhead to Chester (inclusive).

BIRKENHEAD (WOODSIDE).

Restrictions as to Maximum Number of Vehicles on Passenger Trains.—The length of the arrival platforms Nos. 1 and 2 at Woodside are 537 and 534 feet respectively. These figures represent the space available for the use of passengers, but from this distance must be deducted the length of the engine. In calculating the load of a train to Birkenhead the length of the various vehicles forming the train must be considered.

73 feet coaches must not be allowed to stand on No. 3 siding unless they can be on the straight portion beyond the curve.

All trains passing through Woodside Tunnel during the daytime must be lighted up. In the case of stock fitted with electric lighting, where the guard has the means of controlling this whilst running, the light must be switched on immediately before entering the tunnel and switched off immediately after passing out. On other electrically lighted trains lights must be turned on and off at Birkenhead and Rock Ferry.

On gas fitted trains in the down direction, coaches must be lighted up and put on the bye-passes at Chester, and turned on at Rock Ferry. In the up direction gas fitted trains must be fully lighted up at Birkenhead, and turned off at Rock Ferry.

Treadle Gong, Woodside Tunnel.—A treadle gong is fixed on the down line inside the tunnel 30 yards on the Town Station side of the disc home signals, to give to drivers an indication of their position.

Trains being drawn out of Bays at Woodside.—In cases where trains arriving at Woodside are drawn out by an engine attached in the rear, the engine working the train in must not be drawn back with the latter, but it must be detached and remain where detached until the train has been drawn clear of the platform, and the signal lowered for the engine to proceed.

Under no circumstances must an engine be signalled out against an empty train standing on the outgoing line in the tunnel.

Nos. 3 and 6 Lines, Woodside.—The departure from these lines is controlled by means of a disc, and when the latter is taken off for an engine, or engine and vehicles, to proceed, the driver must accept the signal as permission for shunting operations only, and must not, under any circumstances, go right away without first stopping at the signal box and obtaining verbal authority, together with a green hand-signal, from the signalman to proceed to the next block post.

Electric Gong—No. 2 Line—Woodside.—An electric gong is fixed on a pillar between Nos. 2 and 3 roads for the purpose of communicating with the signalman when the points are required to be set for No. 3 line, and drivers are instructed that they must not use engine whistles for the purpose of intimating to the signalman that the points are required to be reversed. A card of instructions is exhibited on the wall adjoining the buffer stops.

BIRKENHEAD TOWN.

Catch Points.—Drivers when stopping at the Birkenhead Town up home signal must be careful to prevent any rebound of their train, otherwise there will be a danger of the coaches leaving the rails should they not be through the catch points.

GREEN LANE JUNCTION.

Engines on to shed.—Where there is only one engine going on to the shed, drivers must see that their firemen give the clearance signal as shown on the code fixed on the signal.

When there are two or more engines going together, the duty will devolve on the man in charge of the last engine, irrespective of which shed it is for, or of the destination of the engines preceding, and in such cases the signal must not be given by any other engineman.

The signal given will be accepted by the signalman as an intimation that the line is absolutely clear.

The safe and efficient operation of any railway required the preparation of detailed instructions, those for the Birkenhead Joint section alone running to 41 pages – almost a page a mile! Enthusiasts often forget the existence of such a mass of rules, and we reproduce a single page from the 1933 Joint instructions.

From Dean to Diesel

The Edwardian era witnessed a transformation from the outside framed engines and gas-lit clerestory stock of the Dean era to the foundations of the 'modern' Great Western. Contemporary views on the Birmingham main line are rare, but to open this section upon the changing face of motive power, we present five scenes, all taken circa 1910 around Leamington Spa.

Above The '36xx' 2-4-2Ts were a feature of the Birmingham suburban services for over thirty years, half the class being allocated there for much of their career. No. 3625 is depicted coupled to a carriage in the short-lived brown livery, replaced in 1912-13 by overall 'lake'.

Below The twenty '39xx' 2-6-2Ts, converted from "Dean Goods" 0-6-0s in 1907-10, were another GWR essay in suburban tank design, and scarcely a very prepossessing one! No. 3905 recalls the lines of these strange conversions. Most were allocated to the Birmingham area. The coach, No. 2692, is an 1895 diagram T34 Brake/3rd 4-wheeler, in brown livery. It was to survive to BR days!

The 3232 class Dean 2-4-0s of 1892-93 were put to work on the cross-country express routes, but were displaced early in Churchward days on to milk and branch services. Illustrations of them at speed, on the Birmingham main line, are understandably rare. To see No. 3238, with her 'standard goods' Belpaire boiler and unique 4-window spectacle plate is particularly exciting. She is passing the south end carriage sidings at Leamington.

No. 2910 *Lady of Shalott,* the last drop-framed 'Saint' to be built in 1906, prior to the introduction of the curved front ends, pauses with an 'up' express at Leamington Spa c1910. This view, and the previous scene, taken contemporaneously with one another, reflect the dramatic change which was being wrought in GWR motive power. The Dean 2-4-0 was not markedly different from engines running at the dawn of the GWR 'narrow gauge' era. The *Lady* is similar to the classes which were to see out GWR steam. The platform trolley, piled high with luggage recalls travel in Edwardian days.

No. 405, a 388 class Armstrong 'standard goods' was just "ex-shops" when caught getting a freight under way at Leamington in 1911. She gleams from end to end, and the cleaners have worked hard with tallow to produce the striped effect on her side rods. No. 405 (Swindon Works No. 96) was one of the first batch of Armstrong goods, and lasted until 1926. The leading wagon is Mountsorrel Granite No. 283 – note the 5-pointed star on the end planking.

From a group of pre-1914 scenes, we next move to a portrait of the changing face of motive power on the Birmingham line, from the thirties to the eighties.

Opposite top We commence with a survivor from the Dean era, 'Duke' class 4-4-0, No. 3281 *Cotswold,* at Tyseley on 13th October 1935. A Banbury and Tyseley engine in the twenties and thirties, she was withdrawn in February 1937.

Opposite below 'Loco Only' portraits are often frowned upon, but in this case, we see the classic lines and detail of the Churchward 'marque' so well that we could not resist this study of No. 4018 *Knight of the Grand Cross* at Oxford on a local passenger just after the war. Less than a decade separated this revolutionary machine from *Cotswold,* for she was built in 1908. Her last years were spent at Stafford Road shed, whose SRD code is just visible on the angle iron behind the buffer beam. Note the whistle shield and elbow steampipes.

Overleaf For a railway as consciously stylish as the Great Western, the 'streamlining' inflicted upon Nos. 6014 *King Henry VII* and 5005 *Manorbier Castle* was a bizarre aberration. No. 5005 is seen at Leamington during the summer of 1935, with full shrouding. This 'Castle' was modified in March 1935, but lost the tender cowling (which must have made coaling a nightmare) in September, and the cylinder and front end fairings followed in due course. More bits went in 1943, and she was restored virtually to original state in 1947. One has to be grateful that the beautiful lines of Collett's 'Castles' were not all treated so.

The last significant group of steam engines to come to the Birmingham line were the BR Standards. The design was split amongst the various works, Swindon being 'parent' for the '82xxx' Class 3 2-6-2Ts, which made their debut in 1952, in which year we see No. 82001.

Above The diesel age precipitated mass withdrawals of steam. Many 'first generation' diesel locomotives and multiple units have made the same journey to oblivion, but others such as No. M51887, leading Driving Motor Brake Second in a 'Derby Suburban' 4-car unit, soldier on. It is seen at High Wycombe in August 1988, 28 years after the class first appeared.

Below After a long spell of 'corporate image' thinking, a spate of area and sector liveries burst upon the railway scene in the 1980s. An initial "Railfreight" grey was replaced by the various sub-sector liveries, and No. 47119 *Arcidae* of the Petroleum sub-sector is newly-bedecked in the latest fashion as it hurries south through Gobowen on 25th August 1988. Men working on the station restoration can be seen on the roof behind the locomotive.

Rebirth of a Station

The dramatic reconstruction of the GWR station at Leamington Spa just before the war has been described in several books in recent years, but illustrations have tended to be of the 'before' and 'after' variety. Over the next five pages, we show just what it all meant.

Above right The old station dated from 1852-53, and had received piecemeal additions over the decades, together with the removal of the Brunellian train shed above the tracks. The station approach was on the 'down' side, that at the eastern end being well below rail level, but infilling and the natural lie of the land allowed the western end of the forecourt to be at rail level, the two sections being connected by a steep ramp. A subway led from the GWR station forecourt to the North Western station forecourt, and also to the 'up' GWR booking office and platform. 'Down' side passengers walked up the slope or the flight of steps. A gigantic Union Castle Line poster advertises the Imperial seaway to South Africa.

The 'down' side booking office, early in 1937. With the imminent demise of the old station, the buildings have been allowed to get into a deplorable state with peeling paint, cracked rendering and missing slates. The low pitched roof, windows flanked by pilasters and cornices suggest railway classicism.

E. C. Jordan & Son of Newport received a contract worth almost £20,000 to reconstruct the subway, excavate the forecourt to low level, and build retaining walls, the approaches and the platform canopies. By the autumn of 1937, their excavator had bitten deep into the high ground outside the 'down' buildings. At first a narrow way was left along the side of the buildings, 'protected' by movable railings, the supports for which are perilously close to the precipice!

Within a few weeks, the western portion of the 'down' buildings had gone, and the ground had been excavated here as well. Part of the building one end filled in with galvanised corrugated sheeting, survived as did the east end pavilion. It is to be hoped that the door from the surviving part of the building on to the former forecourt was securely bolted, for anyone leaving in a hurry would have been in for an unpleasant surprise! We can see the foundations and roof beams of the 1853 buildings, and details of the construction of the Brunellian train shed.

Holliday & Greenwood were given a £35,353 contract to erect the new buildings and platform alterations in 1937. Once the central part of the 1853 station had been cut back still further, they began erecting their girder framework from the west end. Even more ground has been cut away by the far pavilion, and a temporary booking office stands in the 'forecourt'. It will be noticed that the supports for the new building are pre-fabricated, and numbered *Col. 16, 17, 18, 19* etc, to facilitate on site assembly.

Looking from the roadway to the east pavilion, now right at the edge of the excavations, and the temporary booking office. The remains of the subway canopy are visible to the left of the temporary office. Comparison of this view with the upper photograph on page 139 will help locate the various features.

Whilst the forecourt was being excavated, the 'down' platform shelter was demolished and the steelwork for the new canopy erected. No. 4116, 2-6-2T, pauses with a local during this phase of the work. To the right of the canopy is the truncated end of the main section of the building, with its galvanised cladding.

A slice was cut out of the 'up' shelter and awning to permit work to begin on that side. The structural steelwork is in situ for the 'down' canopy.

Once the central section of the 'up' canopy had gone, work shifted to the remaining five sections of the canopy at the Birmingham end of the station. The roofing was removed preparatory to felling the structure. During the whole of this time, the station had to continue to function, as we see from sundry passengers, some luggage on the seat in the midst of the demolition, and No. 4996 *Eden Hall* in the far platform.

With much of the 'up' side cleared, it was possible to start assembling the steelwork for the new canopy. At this time, the residual facilities in the nine bays of structure at the London end of the platform were all that was available. The Leamington Spa sign to the left of the picture is a survival from the old station, and helps locate the relative positions of the old and new canopies. It was a few feet from the Birmingham side of the old and new structures.

On the 'down' side, Holliday & Greenwood were making progress with the main building block, and structural steelwork now extended almost to the east end pavilion. The west wing of the new building was to be two storeys high, and the brick infill and limestone facing is in place. The forecourt level of the main block was to project forwards, and the massive transverse joist at the east end is visible. Some of the brick infill is in situ, and there has been progress with the limestone cladding here too. On the 'up' side, the new canopy (visible through the girders of the 'down' building) has received its covering, and the 9-bay remnant at the east end still survives (visible to the left of the pavilion).

The third storey of the main block is now starting to materialise, and the brick infill advances steadily. The main block, eventually to have nine window bays, is limited to seven at this stage, for the last two cannot be completed until the near pavilion is demolished. The steelwork for the forecourt awning, which projects out in front of the extended forecourt level of the main block, has been erected.

The frontage of the west wing and first seven bays of the main block are complete, but daylight shining through some of the second floor windows, and the ladder above the 'L' of GREAT WESTERN RAILWAY reveal it is still just the façade. The pavilion is still standing, but will soon be demolished. In the foreground, we note the gradient of the road, and see how it was that the east end of the forecourt was well below track level, whilst this end was at track height.

The pavilion has now succumbed, and structural steel work for the last two window bays on the main building is rising up in its place. The temporary wooden booking office is still on site, but the last remnants of the semi-circular awning over the old subway entrance have gone. A superb selection of classic enamelled iron advertisements recall a long lost advertising technique. It includes two Virol plates, one for Petter Oil Engines "Thousands in Use"; a Stephens Ink, four Mazawattee Tea plates, and four Veno's Cough Cure! The last fragment of the 'up' side building still survives, visible between the new structure and the Jordan site hut on the 'down' platform.

The main block on the 'down' side is complete; the entrance to the subway has been rebuilt and clad with limestone blocks, and it will soon be time to remove the forecourt booking office. Other than for incidentals, such as landscaping the area to the right of the subway entrance, the project is virtually complete, and a brand new station has arisen on the site. Our portrait has covered a period of a little under two years, from early in 1937 to late 1938. The Great Western had ambitious plans in mind for further station renewals, but the outbreak of war in 1939 wrote 'finis' to such ideas, and in the few years left to the company after the war, efforts had to be directed to arrears of maintenance. A hundred years on from Brunel, this was the blueprint for the New Great Western which was never to come to pass.

Finale

As the afternoon shadows lengthen, 'Bulldog' class 4-4-0 No. 3448 *Kingfisher* storms up the grade through Southam Road & Harbury station in 1938. The leading wagon, a Stewarts and Lloyds Ltd timber-bodied hopper reminds us that this was the Great Western main line where regular and summer Saturday expresses rubbed shoulders with coal trains, iron ore trains, car transporters and general goods. We hope you have enjoyed this tour of a proud main line, which was created in the face of every difficulty, but which for a myriad of reasons, has long been a Cinderella of the Great Western Railway.